TEN MOST WANTED

TEN MOST WANTED

BRITAIN'S TOP UNDERCOVER COP REINVESTIGATES TEN OF THE UK'S WORST UNSOLVED MURDERS

PETER BLEKSLEY

JOHN BLAKE

Published by John Blake Publishing Ltd,
3 Bramber Court, 2 Bramber Road,
London W14 9PB, England

www.blake.co.uk

First published in hardback in 2005

ISBN 1 84454 149 5

British Library Cataloguing-in-Publication Data:

A catalogue record for this book is available from the British Library.

Design by www.envydesign.co.uk

Printed in Great Britain by William Clowes Ltd, Beccles, Suffolk

1 3 5 7 9 10 8 6 4 2

Papers used by John Blake Publishing are natural, recyclable products made from wood
grown in sustainable forests. The manufacturing processes conform to the
environmental regulations of the country of origin.

This book is dedicated to my three wonderful sons, Brad,
Jack and Ben, who unwittingly and unkowningly provide me
with inspiration and motivation. You guys are my life.

And it is further dedicated to the memory of Wayne, Alex, Riley,
Chinadu, Joan, Les, Milly, the unknown man, Jan and Terry.
Rest in peace

PROLOGUE

There are on average about a thousand murders each year in the United Kingdom. And each year the police capture 90 per cent of the people responsible for these crimes, give or take the odd percentage point. This means that every year up to a hundred murderers get away with their deeds and are free to mingle with the rest of us as we go about our lives. I find this disturbing.

I was puzzled as to why so many cases go unsolved. After all, the police apply vast resources to a murder inquiry, and advances in forensic science mean they have tools at their disposal that Sherlock Holmes could only have dreamed about. I wondered if the murderers were getting smarter; I wanted to know how they came to be one step ahead of the law. So I decided to do something about it and to look into some unsolved cases.

I feel reasonably qualified to do this. I spent over 20 years in the force, most of that time working as a detective. I have caught murderers. I even pretended to be a murderer when working undercover. Some of the informants who supplied me with valuable information over the years ended up being the victims of murder themselves. And for a long time I lived in the shadow of death when some extremely dangerous criminals decided that they wanted to add my name to the statistics.

Armed with a notebook and pencil, a tape recorder and a mobile phone, I set off to see what I could find out. The victims of the crimes I looked into ranged from 13 to 83 years old. They were male, female, black, white and Asian. Some were vicious criminals, while others were law-abiding retired folk. Their deaths came in a variety of ways, from stabbing to shooting, beating, suffocation or burning. But what they all have in common is that their killers are still out there.

I believe I have made significant inroads in these cases. On one occasion I ended up confronting a man in a pub car park and accusing him of being a cold-blooded executioner. I have visited the scenes of the crimes, interviewed grieving parents, and obtained information that has not previously been in the public domain. I have not always made myself popular. Some police forces have welcomed me with open arms, but the majority of them have wished I would go away and leave 'their' crimes alone. The police may investigate them, but these are our crimes as well. They affect our lives and communities. Once you've read about these crimes, you may even want to take up the challenge of being a DIY sleuth yourself. Send me your views and opinions, and if you have any further information, by all means pass it on to me.

The police have had their chance to solve these cases, now let's all have a go and see if we can get some of the most wanted murderers in the land off our streets and where they belong – in prison.

ACKNOWLEDGEMENTS

Many people have helped me with this book, some who must remain anonymous. To those I cannot name, may I say a huge thank you.

To the three wonderful women without whom I could not have completed this project, namely my wife, my mother and the brilliant Hilary Norrish, I send love and thanks.

Along the way, many people have provided a few kind words of encouragememnt, others accommodation and refreshment. Your help was invaluable and I am very fortunate to have you as friends.

Finally, I would like to place on record my my immense gratitude to John Blake for believing I could do this and to all his fantastic staff, including the late James Ravenscroft who was so tragically taken from us in the springtime of his life.

CONTENTS

CHAPTER ONE

'STOP IT, STOP IT, LEAVE HIM ALONE'

The residents of Dales Path were woken by desperate screams. As they peered from their bedroom windows they saw a truly horrific sight. Wayne Trotter, their 30-year-old neighbour, was ablaze. He was frantically trying to summon up help as his flesh, hair and clothing burned. Some people bravely came to his aid. One applied a wet towel, while another doused him with saucepans of water. Someone ran to Wayne's nearby home to tell his wife Anne what was happening. She rushed to her husband while the bearer of the bad news stayed to baby-sit the Trotters' three-year-old child. He was asleep and oblivious to the horror that had befallen his dad. As a trained nurse, Anne did all she could while the gathered crowd awaited the arrival of the emergency services.

Wayne was heard to say, 'They threw something at me. I was blinded. I am in a lot of pain. I am hurting.' An ambulance rushed him to Barnet General Hospital but the nature and severity of his wounds were such that he was soon transferred to a specialist burns unit at the Chelsea and Westminster Hospital. Despite their best efforts to save him, Wayne died 12 hours later.

Situated three miles inside the London orbital motorway, the M25, is the Hertfordshire town of Borehamwood. It was here that I started looking into the cases that make up this book. Borehamwood is an unremarkable town that reminded me of Bexleyheath, the town in which I was brought up. It has a high street with a mix of shops – nationally known retailers, independent traders, charity shops, and the all-too-familiar supermarket. The town has a population of 30,000 people living in 12,000 households. These are a mixture of privately owned, rented and local authority housing.

My first port of call was the office of a local newspaper. I wanted to see if I could find out any useful information about Wayne that they might have had but had not been able to publish. Newspapers are often prevented from publishing details for legal reasons and are sometimes asked to withhold information by the police. I was greeted with tea and enthusiasm by a delightful, young female reporter who was learning her trade before perhaps moving on to greater journalistic heights. Her older, more experienced and somewhat staid editor soon joined us. They were very keen to find out what I was proposing to do and what I hoped to achieve. They filled me in on everything they knew, and for the first time I realised the incredibly strong desire of local people to see this crime solved. As I left, armed with some useful knowledge, I thanked them for their help and promised to keep them informed of my findings.

Wayne and Anne enjoyed a happy marriage as far as I could establish. They were eagerly looking forward to the birth of their second child. Anne was six months pregnant when, in the early hours of Thursday, 5 December 2002, Wayne was making his way home from work as usual. He had just finished a late shift at the Renolit plastics factory in Cricklewood, north-west London, where he was employed as a team leader. He had worked there for many years, as did his father Bill.

Wayne left the factory shortly after 11pm and took a Thameslink train from Hendon to Borehamwood and Elstree station. He then caught a bus to take him the ten-minute journey to where Barnet Lane meets Furzehill Road. After getting off, he walked into the Farriers Estate where he lived. By now it was about 12.30am. It is believed that he then walked along Farriers Way, a road that leads into the centre of the estate, and towards the Farriers Estate community centre. At, or near to, the centre he was attacked, doused with petrol, and set alight.

As news of this horrific attack spread, a sense of shock and revulsion was felt by the residents of the estate and the police alike. Detective Superintendent Steve Read of the Hertfordshire Constabulary, who was tasked with leading the inquiry, said, 'This was an appalling and ferocious attack on a local family man and it appears completely motiveless.' He continued, 'This is the most violent random attack that I have ever seen, and whoever was responsible for it must be brought to justice at all costs.' He urged anyone with information to come forward.

The unusual nature of this killing ensured national publicity. Reporters descended upon the area in their droves, including television film crews. A mobile police unit was set up on the

3

estate, an incident room was established, and detectives set about their inquiries. Some items were recovered at, or near to, the scene of the crime. They were a green plastic petrol can, a stick with a sock tied around one end, a partially burned pink glove with three of the fingers cut off and these were found nearby, a Stanley knife without the blade protruding, and a white baseball cap with a C&G (Cheltenham & Gloucester Building Society) logo printed on the front, consisting of white letters on a blue background. It appeared to have been damaged by fire. These findings were not made public by the police for more than a year.

Any decision as to what information may or may not be released to the public via the media is made by the senior investigating officer, the head of the inquiry. Sometimes information regarding wounds inflicted on a victim is withheld so that in the event of a person confessing to the crime, the authenticity of that confession can be confirmed. Bizarre as it may seem, some odd characters will confess to crimes that they did not commit. Furthermore, if the police are dealing with a murder that they suspect may be linked to other similar crimes, they may withhold information until such linkage is proved beyond doubt.

In this case, though there may have been a good reason, I remain puzzled as to why the details of the items found were not released at the time. They would appear to be crucial clues and worthy of being put into the public domain at the earliest possible stage, when people's recollection of events was still fresh in their minds.

Four days after the killing, with the inquiry in full swing, Wayne's mum Vicki Cooledge made the first of what for her were to be many press appeals. Through her tears and grief she was able to say, 'Every mother out there knows what I am going through and knows that they not only killed Wayne, they killed me too.' She offered a chilling thought: 'Remember, if they don't come to justice, it could be your child next.' Jeff Kagan, who was the operations manager at Renolit, was also present at the press conference. He had known Wayne since he was a boy and spoke of the shock all of the staff at the factory were feeling.

Another of the senior police officers on the inquiry, Detective Chief Inspector Adrian Tapp, revealed that the police wanted to trace some young people seen in the area at the time of the attack on Wayne. No other details were forthcoming, but he said, 'It is quite possible that not all of those three or four youths were involved, and if they weren't, they were horrified by what their friends did. We are asking them to search their souls and come forward.' This would not be the last time that the police appealed to people's consciences.

Less than two miles from Borehamwood are the famous Elstree Film and Television Studios. Numerous screen classics have been made there, including Agatha Christie's *Murder on the Orient Express*. The area has benefited financially from the presence of the studios for many years, and when they were put up for sale by their owners in 1996 there was a very real threat that the site might be purchased and put to some other use. As an indication of their importance to the local people, it was Hertsmere Borough Council who stepped in and bought the site, pledging to guarantee its continued use as studios. They have been true to their word. Directors from Elstree donated £500 to an appeal fund set up in Wayne's name. Any money raised would go to benefit Anne, her son and the baby that was due soon.

Shortly after Christmas, Vicki was again making an appeal via the media. She appealed to those who knew what had happened. 'I understand they must be petrified because of the repercussions, but this cannot go unpunished, and as long as I live I will be fighting this. All we have got is the public, and someone has got some information out there. It is like living a hell. Half of me keeps going for Anne and the little one, but inside I feel totally empty.' Wayne was described as a family-loving man who enjoyed cooking, football and golf. Like many people of his age and circumstances, he would talk of his plans for the future. Tragically, Vicki told that at Christmas, 'The little one was calling out for his daddy.' Detective Superintendent Read said of the inquiry, 'It is hard work, but we are still confident that the answer to this murder lies on the estate.'

A month on and no arrests had been made. 'Wall of silence' was an expression being used more and more, both in the media and by the local people. Councillor Stuart Nagler, the Mayor of Hertsmere, decided to try to do his bit. He announced that he was to visit schools, community centres and youth clubs in an effort to stress to youngsters the importance of reporting anything they knew. He also handed out a telephone number on which he could be contacted if people wanted to speak to him in confidence.

Detective Superintendent Read again appealed to those who had information but who might be scared to come forward. 'I can reassure them that we have vast experience in making sure people remain safe in these situations,' he said. Local residents were concerned about their safety, and some spoke of setting up a neighbourhood watch scheme, but as I later discovered this idea never got off the ground. Some such schemes have been successful in reducing crime and antisocial behaviour in neighbourhoods up and down the country. When I moved into my current house I was asked by a neighbour if I wanted to join our local scheme. I was in the police at the time and, being a hard-nosed, battle-weary and cynical detective, I was a little unsure of their usefulness. In recent years my opinion has changed, and, while still not a signed-up member, my dear neighbour keeps me informed of any local problems and puts a newsletter through my door from time to time.

In May 2003, an unnamed 33-year-old man from Borehamwood was arrested on suspicion of committing Wayne's murder. No details were released by police, however, and it was four months before this information became public. He was released without charge and bailed to return to a police station in September.

Six months after the attack the police had still not charged anyone, so they made another public appeal. Detective Superintendent Read said, 'We have built up a very good picture of what happened on the night Wayne was attacked. But the final pieces of the puzzle need putting together and we are again appealing for anyone with information to come forward.' He went on to say that a couple, described as being in their late 20s to early 30s, had been seen walking a large white or beige dog near to where the attack happened. The lady was described as being tall with blonde hair. They had not yet been traced and he asked for them to make contact.

He appeared more concerned, however, with speaking to someone to whom he delivered a strongly worded message: 'We believe there was at least one person who was present at the time Wayne was attacked who played no part in the incident and did not like what they saw. We need that person to come forward and tell us what happened and explain why we should treat them differently to the others who we identify as having been present.'

From this it appeared that the net was closing in on those responsible. Detective Superintendent Read was saying clearly that the police believed they knew the identities of some of the persons present. Indeed it could be construed that they knew who had actually set Wayne alight. I was surprised, therefore, that having declared he knew of this person who had apparently taken no part in the attack, Read should deliver a message to them that could be interpreted as threatening. This person could be the vital piece of the puzzle. If they were to come forward, they would in all likelihood become the crucial witness for the prosecution in any trial. Surely a more sympathetic approach, one designed to encourage this person to come over to the side of righteousness, might have been more appropriate and more likely to achieve the desired response. What was to be gained by saying this person would have to explain himself? But the police must have felt this was an effective method of dealing with recalcitrant youths.

A £10,000 reward was now being offered for information that led to the conviction of those responsible. The stakes were rising. I wonder if the police felt their chances of solving this case were slipping away from them.

By this time Anne had given birth to a daughter who would never know her dad. When 10 September 2003 arrived, the man arrested in May duly answered his bail. He was taken into custody, along with three other people who had also been arrested that day in an operation carried out by murder squad detectives. The investigation had now been named Operation Refit. The others arrested were a 24-year-old man, and two women aged 26 and 19, all of whom were described as coming from the Borehamwood area. Their ages suggest that the police had changed tack from searching for 'youths', who they had spoken of in previous appeals.

DCI Tapp made a brief statement in which he adopted a reassuring tone for any potential witness, echoing the message of his boss, Detective Superintendent Read, the previous January. He said, 'Although today's arrests are a significant step in the investigation process, we still need people to ring us with any information they have. All calls are treated in the strictest confidence, and we have much experience at protecting witnesses if this is necessary.' He concluded, 'If you do have information, please come forward and tell us what you know.'

The media, not surprisingly, reported these arrests as a breakthrough in the investigation, but on 14 September the police announced that all four persons arrested had been released without charge but were bailed to return to police stations in December.

As the one-year anniversary of Wayne's murder approached, police launched a fresh publicity campaign. Door-to-door enquiries were also renewed. The BBC television programme *Crimewatch* decided to include the case in its episode due for transmission on 18 December 2003. A reconstruction of Wayne's last movements was filmed with an actor playing the part of the victim. Residents of Dales Path who had helped him as he burned also contributed. For the first time the police showed the public replicas and photographs of the petrol can, the stick with the sock tied to it, (they described the sock as 'material'), the Stanley knife and the baseball cap that had been found. They said that they needed to establish who these belonged to.

The dog walkers with the white or beige dog who had been mentioned previously in the six-month anniversary appeal were also featured on *Crimewatch*. They were later identified, not as a result of the programme but through the fresh door-to-door inquiries on the estate. During my research into this case and others, I have spoken to many dog owners when they have been out exercising their pets. My respect for these people has increased significantly. They have always been keen to help, and possess an acute level of awareness of their surroundings.

On *Crimewatch*, the police appealed once again to the conscience of their vital missing witness. Now they were being more specific about this person and what they were believed to have said. After a general appeal for witnesses, DCI Tapp said, 'In particular we need to hear from a woman or girl who was heard to scream "stop it, stop it, leave him alone" just prior to residents discovering Wayne on fire. This person is likely to know the identity of Wayne's killers, and I appeal to you directly to come forward. If it's you, please contact us. If you are scared, I would like to reassure you that we have vast experience at protecting witnesses. Please look to your conscience and think about the effect this is having on Wayne's family.'

Later in the programme, Tapp spoke again, but appeared to abandon his tactic of appealing to the consciences of people in order to adopt a rather more forceful tone. It seemed he was using the tried and trusted psychological trick of the good cop, bad cop routine, but playing both roles himself. He said, 'We are determined and confident we will solve this murder inquiry, but we still need anyone with information to come forward, and if you were present at the time Wayne was attacked, my advice to you is come to us before we come to you.'

Around twenty calls were received by the inquiry team as a result of the TV appeal, a response described by Tapp as 'solid'. New lines of inquiry were followed up.

So what of the four people arrested in September, who had been bailed to return to police stations in December? The police made no mention of them then, nor have they done so since. All went quiet from both police and media for the next 12 months, until 3 December 2004, two days short of the second anniversary of Wayne's murder. Now was the time for the inquest into his death to be held. Coroner Edward Thomas heard the evidence at Hatfield Petty Sessions Court. He was told that Wayne received burns to 90 per cent of his body, which proved fatal. A verdict of unlawful killing was returned. The coroner expressed considerable sympathy for Wayne's family and said he was pleased the police inquiry was still open.

Detective Inspector Liz Hannon represented the murder squad at this hearing, and appeared on the lunchtime regional television news. She also made reference to the witness heard to say 'stop it, stop it, leave him alone', but said that it could have been a female or a high-pitched male voice that uttered those words.

In early 2005, I decided to inform the Hertfordshire Constabulary of my interest in this case. I didn't, after all, want to do something that might interfere with what they were doing, nor did I want to jeopardise any possible future trials. In fact, I thought they might be grateful for the publicity my book may generate, and that they might perhaps meet me to discuss the case. Certain members of the Hertfordshire Constabulary later proved that my thinking had been entirely wrong, and that they regarded my interest in this case as less than welcome.

I made numerous phone calls and sent many emails to their press office, which is delightfully entitled the 'Corporate Communications Department', without getting any reply. After five weeks of persistence, I finally got word from them saying they could not assist me. Undaunted, I continued with my research, while thinking how short-sighted their attitude was.

Unhelpful is not a word I could use to describe the vast majority of people who live on the Farriers Estate. The community centre seemed like an obvious place to pay a visit. It is an L-shaped brick building situated in the middle of the estate, and as I approached it I saw a notice board on the outside wall. It was dominated by a large appeal poster featuring a picture and the words of Anne, who by now had returned to her native Ireland with the children. It read, 'A loving husband and father is missing from our lives and we still do not know why.' Clearly this community was not going to forget easily. A smaller notice was stuck inside a window informing people that a Tsunami appeal fund had been set up by the residents.

I had seen two grey-haired ladies enter the centre so I decided to knock on the door and make my way in. The moment I introduced myself and explained what I was doing, any concerns that I harboured of experiencing animosity or unpleasantness instantly disappeared. From then on, virtually every resident that I spoke to on the estate was pleasant, as helpful as they could be, and united in hoping that this book would help in some way in bringing Wayne's killers to justice. I was beginning to feel a certain degree of responsibility about it all.

Everybody I spoke to agreed Wayne was a good man. He worked hard and loved his family. He and his family were described as quiet, in that they kept themselves to themselves. However, the more people I spoke to, the more a picture of Wayne began to emerge that you wouldn't have guessed from any of the previously released information. To many of the locals he was something of a hero. Why? Because if he saw any youths getting up to no good, he would confront them and tell them what he thought of them and their antisocial behaviour. Not for Wayne the fear of retribution, of having your house daubed with graffiti, or your car vandalised. No, he would give them a piece of his mind. This did not make him popular with some of the more troublesome elements on the estate. But as a father of a three-year-old, and with another on the way, maybe he wanted the Farriers Estate to be a decent place to raise his young family.

Construction of the Farriers Estate started in 1975. The site was previously a stables complex where local people would bring their children to interact with the horses. The equine link meant that for the first few years of its existence the estate was known as the 'Horses House Estate', before the official name became more commonly used. Most of the street names have a link to horses, hence Cob Close, Saddlers Way, and so on.

People who have lived there since it opened are known as 'originals', although their numbers are now dwindling as the occupants get ever older. One such 'original' I spoke to told me of the problems with crime that existed even before most people had moved on to the estate, namely that as building materials were delivered to the site by day, they would disappear as quickly by night. This contributed to the construction company going broke before completing the estate, so the local council stepped in to ensure the project was finished.

This meant that the council then had possession of an entire estate that it had not anticipated, so when Margaret Thatcher was Prime Minister and introduced her controversial 'right to buy' policy for council house residents, they were encouraged to purchase their homes. Some did, many did not, and the remaining authority-owned dwellings, and the overall running and maintenance of the estate, are the responsibility of a privately owned company.

My first impression of the Farriers Estate was good. Sure the grass verges were in need of some attention, and there was some litter and graffiti, but nothing that a task force of volunteers or housing association employees could not put right in a day or two.

But there is no newsagents or general store on the estate, which is something I found disappointing. In my experience of estates, and I've worked on some of the largest and most deprived in the country, such a shop can provide a focal point where people often meet by chance, exchange pleasantries, discuss local matters, interact with the owner, and generally enhance the sense of community so important to any neighbourhood.

Such a shop had existed up until a few years previously. The Asian owner was apparently well liked by the majority of residents. But he was hounded out of business by shoplifting, robberies and persistent break-ins. The more measures he put in place to combat these crimes, the more the criminals found ways around them. When he went to the considerable expense of fitting state-of-the-art security shutters on the front of the building, burglars went in through the roof. This was the last straw, so he sold up and left.

The building was then taken over and converted into a pre-school nursery, which it is today. The company that runs the nursery has an extremely good reputation in the world of pre-school education, consequently people bring their children from miles around. This is borne out by the number of cars that compete for the few parking spaces available in front of it. So a building that was previously utilised almost exclusively by the local residents is now used by people with few links to the community.

The nursery and the community centre are next to one another, divided by a four-metre-wide pathway that runs into Dales Path, and the row of five terraced houses where Wayne sought help. The walls of this pathway are decorated on the community centre side by a large mural depicting an idyllic housing scene, complete with trees and greenery, blue skies and birds. This was painted by children from the estate, and unveiled by the local Mayor in 2001. On the nursery side, windows have been painted with pictures of dolphins, the sun, the moon and stars. It was down this pathway, and between these images, that family man Wayne took his last steps before being attacked.

The pathway ends and Dales Path and begins at the rear of these buildings. Behind are a number of places where people could lie in wait preparing to commit a crime. A short walkway to the rear door of the nursery could provide cover for would-be felons, as could a fenced area and some bushes behind the community centre. This fenced area houses the rubbish bins for the community centre; it measures about nine square metres, and the fencing is six feet high. It is accessed via a gate that is never locked and provides a haunt for youths wishing to smoke or take drugs.

A small triangle of grass extends from the bushes; it is some 15 metres long and is where Wayne finally fell. A sycamore tree stands here, and I noticed a simple wooden cross, the type that you find on Remembrance Day wreaths, in the ground next to it. It bore the word 'Remembrance' and a note that merely read 'The Farriers Residents Association'.

While the bin area and the bushes would provide reasonable cover for anyone not wishing to be seen, they are not the sort of places I would choose to conceal myself if I was about to commit a crime. Being hidden is one thing, but being able to see your intended target and the surrounding environment is equally important. If you are lying in wait, intending to carry out a pre-planned attack on a person who is on foot, you ideally need to be able to see them approach. You need to see if they are alone, and to see if they are carrying anything that could be used as a weapon. You also need to be able to see the pace at which they are moving, in order to ensure that you have ready any weapon you are going to use, and to time your attack in order to make most use of the element of surprise.

If you are about to attack premises, your target will of course be static. It is most important therefore to have your implements for use in the crime ready, and to ensure that your escape route is clear.

From the area where Wayne was attacked I found no less than six possible escape routes, all within 30 metres. These consisted of alleyways, paths and access to roads. These are common features on the Farriers Estate, about which the residents complain endlessly. Most of the estate consists of short terraces of houses or flats, all divided by these alleys and paths, which make it resemble a rabbit warren. They were incorporated into the design of the estate in order to give it a village feel, but they have proved problematic, as anybody misbehaving can easily escape when being challenged or pursued. This has particularly been the case with youths on scooters or motorbikes, and with those who partake in stone throwing, another popular pastime among some groups. On one of my visits to the estate I noticed that railings were being erected in some places in order to tackle this very problem.

The nursery school and the pathway were once overseen by closed-circuit television, but not at the time of the attack on Wayne. The cameras had been erected on brackets only 12 feet high, so the youths found it easy to repeatedly smash them. They also enjoyed throwing objects at the metal box that housed the burglar alarm bell for the nursery. This used to set it off, much to the annoyance of those living nearby.

The community centre had also been subjected to attack in the past. Whenever it was booked for a function that was to incorporate a bar serving alcoholic drinks, it would become a target for burglars. The alcohol being stored for the party was usually what they were after. It had also been subjected to an arson attack not long before the attack on Wayne. A fire was lit at the bottom of the fire escape doors that are situated not at the rear but on a side wall. Before it could cause extensive damage, the fire brigade attended and put it out. The centre had also been damaged by people using it. Attempts had been made some time previously to set up a youth club. It failed because rules, such as no smoking, were enforced by people who the youths could not connect with. Equipment was damaged, and the idea soon abandoned.

One dark January night as I made my way around the estate, I saw five young lads going in and out of the bin area behind the community centre. I decided to keep an eye on them while doing my best not to be seen. I watched as they repeatedly went in and out. After about half an hour they all came out and made their way to an area not far from where a memorial bench to Wayne stands. I decided to approach them. They looked at me a little suspiciously as I got ever closer; it turned out that they thought I might have been local CID. Once they knew who I was and what I was doing, they opened up and spoke. They were aged between ten and fifteen and were all residents of the estate. They were polite and friendly lads.

I asked them what they had been doing in the bin area and they told me they often went there, as it was a cool place to hide. I wasn't entirely convinced by this but it was obvious none of them were on drugs. I soon brought the conversation around to the community centre. 'That's for the old fogies. They don't want us in there,' was the immediate response. They went on to explain that it was regarded as off limits for young people, with no activities for them held there, and consequently it has become a symbol of resentment for the youth of the estate. And one that they cannot ignore as they see it virtually every day of their lives.

We discussed the failed attempts to start a youth club. They told me that if the right people were employed to run such a club, and if the right facilities were made available, such as pool tables, a sound system and affordable refreshments, they felt it would be worth giving it another go. They complained further that a grass area next to the community centre was not to be used for ball games but that it was OK for adults to allow their dogs to mess there. They went on to say that an open area on the edge of the estate only had small five-a-side football goals on it and, in any event, on cold winter nights, football on grass with no floodlights was not seen as fun by many of the youngsters, especially the girls.

The lads went on to say that the estate had become quieter since Wayne's murder. Not so many young people went out at night, consequently vandalism and disorder was less of a problem than before. The large police presence that had been seen on the estate was of course now long gone, but another side effect had been that fewer stolen cars and motorbikes were dumped there. It was good to hear these kids talking positively about improvements to their environment, albeit ones that had come about as a result of a tragedy. As we prepared to part I asked them if they had the opportunity to change one thing about the estate, what it would be. They were unanimous. 'That place,' said the oldest, pointing to the community centre as the others nodded and spoke their agreement. 'It's supposed to be a community centre, right; we're from the community, right; so why aren't we allowed to use it? We're out here with nothing to do. It's empty now. We could be in there having a laugh, instead we're out here bored, just bored.'

The lighting at night on the estate is reasonably good; there's the occasional bulb missing from a lamppost, but generally it is OK, particularly, and surprisingly so, at the scene of the attack. A double lamppost casts much light on the area and is supported by lighting attached to the walls of the community centre. It is matters such as lighting and other crime-preventative measures that concerned many of the residents I spoke to. One of their main wishes was to see more police on the estate, and fewer of them in the high street on a Saturday afternoon when they embark on recruitment drives.

Many residents had theories as to why Wayne was killed. More than one person said a rumour had gone around about him having an affair and that the attack was connected to that. The fact that the people arrested in September 2003 were aged 19, 24, 26 and 33, and that two of them were women, would perhaps add some weight to that theory, but I remain unconvinced. Others said that it was believed he had disturbed someone preparing to siphon, or being in the act of siphoning, petrol from a car. Had this been the case then a length of tubing would have been needed with which to suck the petrol from the tank. This would surely have been found along with the other items such as the petrol can. Besides, stealing petrol in this way is not common these days and is usually carried out by a lone offender. And I think it unlikely a petrol thief would respond so violently to being discovered.

By now I had gathered a lot of information that I needed to analyse. I had also been invited to a forthcoming residents meeting, which was going to be held in the community centre on 16 February. I was told that the senior police officer investigating the case was going to be present, along with other prominent persons involved in matters relating to the estate. It was felt by some of the people that I had spoken to that this might be an opportunity to develop more contacts, get my face known locally, and possibly learn more about Wayne's murder.

Two weeks later I made sure that I arrived early for the 7.30pm meeting. I parked my car and decided to wait in the car park at the front of the centre. People began to arrive, including a smartly dressed man and woman. I walked behind them as they approached the two buildings that are the community centre and the nursery. I heard the man say to his companion, 'Which is the community centre?' It was pointed out to him by the woman. 'And what is this?' he asked as he indicated the building with a large sign saying 'nursery'. I wondered who he could be as he was obviously not familiar with the area.

I followed them in, accepted the offer of a cup of tea, and mingled with some of the people already gathered there. I saw the smartly dressed man and woman disappear into a side room with a lady I had not previously seen. After a few minutes somebody asked me if I had been introduced to Wayne's mum Vicki. I had tried to make contact with her before by way of email but had not been successful. I was, however, still keen to speak to her. I recognised her as the lady that had disappeared into the side room not long before. I approached her and introduced myself, giving her my card and trying to explain my book. I was very aware that I was dealing with a lady who had suffered the unimaginable grief of losing a child, so I was careful in my choice of words.

Not long into our conversation we were joined by the smartly dressed woman from earlier. She came very close to me and asked, 'Who are you?' I told her, gave her my card, and went on to explain what I was doing. She gave me her card. She was Detective Constable Lorraine Harrison, the Family Liaison Officer appointed to look after Vicki. We had a conversation lasting several minutes during which she told me that my interest in the case was not particularly helpful. I asked her to explain why but she declined to tell me.

We took our places for the meeting, which eventually got going at 8pm. It was attended by 35 residents and 14 nonresidents, including me. This was apparently the best turnout for one of these meetings in a long time. Representatives from the local council, the borough council, the housing association, the fire brigade, neighbourhood watch, the police and the local press were all present. The police were particularly well represented with four officers and two civilian employees. A local quipped to me that it would be a good time to go on a crime spree elsewhere in Borehamwood.

After introductions, the man who I had seen outside and who had not known which building was the community centre, rose to speak. He introduced himself as Detective Superintendent Ken Bell and explained that he had taken over the investigation into Wayne's murder, but had only been working on the case for two weeks. He went on to tell the audience that he had transferred to the Hertfordshire Constabulary the previous October from the Metropolitan Police, where he had worked on 'lots of murders'. He stated this was the most horrific murder he had investigated and that an element of luck would be needed to solve it.

When he had finished speaking he took questions from the audience, including one from me. I introduced myself, explained what I was doing and asked him if he would be willing to have a meeting. He said he would, and when the question and answer session ended, he approached me, took my card and said he would call within the next two weeks. Eight weeks later he telephoned me and said he would call me again to arrange a meeting. I am still waiting.

A Mr Derek Sweeney addressed the meeting, and explained that he was the local neighbourhood watch coordinator. He made a well-reasoned, convincing and impassioned plea for people to come forward and help him establish such a scheme on the estate. This idea of course had been mooted by some of the residents soon after Wayne's death. If they get it up and running, and if Mr Sweeney has anything to do with it, I'm sure it will be a success.

Vicki was one of the last people to speak to the audience. I was struck by her bravery in doing so. She read from a pre-prepared speech and was sometimes barely audible, but spoke of the pain she still felt 26 months after the event. She asked for people with information to come forward before another such crime happened to somebody else. She also complained about media interest being non-existent apart from on each anniversary.

Shortly afterwards the meeting came to a close and I mingled once more. On my way out I spoke to Vicki. 'If it's publicity you want, Vicki, give some thought to speaking to me. I might just be able to help.' She smiled and I wished her well.

I then did another of my trips around the estate, checking out the different views of where the attack took place from different vantage points. I retraced Wayne's last steps in an effort to view the scene as he would have done. A theory was beginning to take shape in my head.

I don't believe that whoever killed Wayne that night set out intending to do so. If I was going to kill someone, setting fire to them in an outdoor environment is the last thing I'd do. It's not guaranteed to be successful for starters, an element of restraint may be required in order to sufficiently douse the victim, and there is considerable risk of the assailants getting accidentally doused and therefore injured in the process. If such a splash went on to an attacker's clothing and was not ignited, and if it was detected by the police, it could provide forensic evidence that would be very difficult to argue away in court. In any event, there are many preferred and more successful ways to murder someone, such as shooting, stabbing, beating or even strangling.

I believe the culprits set out that night with no intention of murdering anyone, but intended to set fire to the community centre. I believe that they went equipped with petrol in the can, and the sock tied to the stick, which was a purpose-made and excellent tool with which to daub petrol around the building. Using this tool would have enabled them to spread petrol into parts of the building that would not have been reached by merely splashing it about. They could have done a proper job on it and ensured the building would be destroyed.

Much research has been done into the motivations of those who commit arson, with up to 200 categories outlined. A Home Office paper entitled 'The Arson Scoping Study' identified four main motivation categories. They are:

- Youth disorder and nuisance attacks. This includes acts of vandalism and fires brought on by boredom and thrill seeking.
- Malicious attacks. These include arson attacks driven by the motivations of revenge, racism and clashes of beliefs or rivalries.
- Psychological attacks. This covers fires started by persons suffering from mental illness, and those started by suicidal people.
- Criminal attacks. These include fires started by people in order to conceal another crime, such as theft or murder, and those where people stand to gain financially, such as insurance fraud.

If the intended target that fateful night was indeed the community centre, I believe the offenders could easily be grouped into the youth disorder and nuisance, or the malicious category, depending on their motives.

In any event, if these would-be arsonists were lying in wait at the rear of the community centre, perhaps in the bin storage area or the bushes as I believe they were, this would make sense, as the kitchen window is close by. The kitchen has cupboards and work surfaces all made of combustible materials and would be the best place to start a fire in order to maximise the damage. The main hall, which is on the other side of the centre, is usually cleared at night and contains very little that is readily combustible. There is also no suitable place near to the hall in which to hide while waiting for the right moment in which to break in and start the fire.

So, as Wayne walked home, I believe the would-be arsonists saw him and panicked. They thought that he might be able to identify them to the police, and in an effort to evade capture they used the element of surprise to jump him. A criminal enterprise such as this leads to an inevitable adrenaline rush, and as a result, in a matter of seconds, things got fatally out of hand. With one of them having a petrol can ready to hand, primed with the cap off, and with another holding a cigarette lighter or something similar, these people committed the acts that had such tragic consequences. In a few moments of unplanned madness, they managed to ensure that they would be wanted by the police for the rest of their lives.

So if this was the case, why has the person heard to say 'stop it, stop it, leave him alone' not come forward and enabled the police to bring this case to a close? One reason may be that they are fearful they will not be believed, either by the police or in a court of law.

And what lies in store for this witness if he or she does come forward? If they had entered into any kind of criminal conspiracy or committed any offence in relation to this event, they would have to tell the police and later admit their guilt in court. For example if this person purchased the petrol in order to burn down the community centre but had absolutely no intention of hurting a living soul with it, they would have to be charged with an offence appropriate to their actions – conspiracy to commit criminal damage by fire, for example.

They would also have to make a witness statement detailing fully the activities of themselves and their co-conspirators before, during and after the event. This is evidence that, in the event of their accomplices pleading 'not guilty', they would be required to give in court.

When a 'witness' appears in court charged with an offence they have confessed to, the judge is made aware of their cooperation with police, and passes sentence accordingly. This invariably means that the person receives a hugely reduced punishment. One of my informants was arrested for an extremely serious drugs offence, for which he was looking at anything up to 14 years in jail. When informed of the important work he was doing for me, the judge gave him a suspended sentence.

The protection of such witnesses is of course vital, and we know that Hertfordshire Police, on more than one occasion, spoke of their experience in this field. I have some experience of the Witness Protection Programme and all its pitfalls, because I lived in the system from 1993 to 1995.

My work undercover led me to infiltrate a gang of

international heroin dealers affiliated to a terrorist organisation. When the bad guys delivered a consignment of heroin to me worth £4m, they were arrested. While languishing in jail awaiting their trial, they deduced that I was an undercover cop, and working on the theory that if they killed me, the evidence against them would disappear, they sent messages to the outside world that there was a large sum of cash available to anyone who could put a bullet in my head. This contract on me was discovered by virtue of a phone-tap on a bar in Boston, Massachusetts, being monitored by the FBI.

I had to abandon my home, move into a safe house, live under an assumed name and bid farewell to the identity of Peter Bleksley. Finding somewhere suitable to live, changing car, setting up bank accounts, mortgages, domestic bill accounts, obtaining passports, driving licence, credit cards, National Insurance and tax documentation, all manner of insurances and so on, are all time consuming and far from straightforward. Of course a non-police person will have most of this done for them by the Witness Protection Programme staff, but it is still problematic.

For the police it is an expensive system, but one that is becoming ever more necessary in the increasingly violent society in which we now live. The government has recently put forward a proposal for a nationwide witness protection programme.

The system is often attacked by defence barristers when cases in which such witnesses feature come to trial. They allege that inclusion in the programme is often offered as an inducement by police in exchange for the evidence they want to hear, as opposed to the truth.

Fortunately not all protected witnesses require the level of protection that I did. For many, a panic alarm and CCTV will suffice. In fact, the police like witnesses to stay within their own communities if possible, and to set an example, both to other potential victims and the bad guys, that they will not stand for intimidation and threats.

For the memory of Wayne, for Anne and the children, for his parents and other members of his family, and, last but not least, for the wonderful people of the Farriers Estate, whose neighbourhood remains so affected by this crime, I would love to see this matter brought to a conclusion. Numerous lives, including I suspect those of whoever did this, are in a state of limbo, and people are being prevented from moving on. So if you are the person who said 'stop it, stop it, leave him alone' and you want to speak to someone who is not in the police but knows exactly what could lie in store for you and how best to deal with that, I would ask you to please make contact with me. I am willing to help in any way I can.

CHAPTER TWO

TAXI FOR MR BLUE

I had not been to Glasgow for over 15 years, so as I took my seat on flight GSM991 I was looking forward to seeing if and how the city had changed. Back in the late 1980s I had spent a lot of time there. I had forged a close working relationship with a Scottish undercover detective, and together we became a plausible and successful double act. When he was offered large quantities of drugs or other contraband, he would tell the bad guys that he had a contact 'down south', and likewise I would speak about 'my man in Scotland'. We would perform the necessary introductions and thereafter negotiate to pay for and transport the illicit commodities that were up for sale. The pair of us would explain how we liked to do business with trustworthy fellow criminals who came from out of our home cities, so that other local and potentially competing crooks would not know the sources of our wares and would be unable to muscle in on our business. This scam worked a treat.

I became well known at the London headquarters of a major Scottish bank, as I often visited their vaults to book out huge quantities of Scottish bank notes with which to 'pay' for whatever I was supposed to be buying. The criminals of course did not get the money, instead they usually ended up having to serve lengthy jail terms a long way from home.

'Jimmy', as the villains came to know my cohort, and I would compete with one another to provide the best hospitality at the end of any triumphant operation. Very little was off limits as we introduced each other to various hostelries and acquaintances who would be most accommodating of our long and often vocal celebrations. Nevertheless, my abiding memories of Glasgow were that of a dark city, both to look at and to experience, where violence seemed to be lurking, ready to pounce upon the Sassenach should I show disrespect or get ideas above my station.

A bright and sunny day greeted me as I loaded my luggage into the taxi that was to take me to my hotel. Under normal circumstances as a cheaper alternative I would have caught a train, but taxis were to feature large in my time in Glasgow, and, as luck would have it, this driver knew much about the case I was here to research.

On Tuesday, 25 June 2002 at about 12.40am, an ambulance attended 3 Dundonald Road, Dowanhill. This is one of the most salubrious parts of Glasgow. The emergency services had been called by neighbours, and when they arrived they found 41-year-old Alexander Blue lying in the driveway. He was suffering from severe head wounds as the result of a beating, and the paramedics set about doing all they could to keep him alive. He was taken to hospital where staff spent the next two days trying to save him, but a surgeon who treated him was later heard to say, 'They didn't leave us a lot to work on.' He died two days later.

Dundonald Road became a hive of police activity as lighting and canopies were erected and the white-suited forensic experts set about their business. Neighbours who had previously slept through events were awoken by this activity. They were soon to be visited by police performing house-to-house inquiries.

The media began to theorise and speculate about who could have been responsible. They had a lot of material to work on as Alex Blue had led anything but a straightforward life. His childhood, however, had given no indication that his life would become such a web of intrigue. He was born the middle of three sons to his working-class parents in Glasgow. His elder brother Billy was three years his senior, and his younger brother Gavin was three years his junior. Alex was described to me as an 'average' youngster. He had various hobbies: stamp collecting, going to nightclubs where he enjoyed dancing, and football. He was a hopeless outfield player but excelled as a goalkeeper. Some people thought he was good enough to make a career out of it.

Alex would drop these hobbies as quickly as he took them up, until he started reading car magazines. He read them from cover to cover many times and soon started to buy car price guide publications. He read and absorbed the information avidly. Before long he was able to accurately quote the price of any make and model of car you asked of him. This interest in cars was regarded by his family as just another fad, and he was not drawn to the motor trade when he left school. Instead he became an apprentice electrician, but soon after qualifying he decided to change career, and it was then that he entered the motor trade. It was an industry that was to bring him bankruptcy and, later on, wealth. He worked for various dealerships including those that sold Mercedes and BMWs. He became a polished and slick salesman. While selling these prestige cars he met many professional people, such as lawyers, accountants and businessmen, with whom he liked to socialise. Alex hardly ever drank alcohol and did not smoke. He shunned smoky pubs and preferred to frequent coffee shops and bistros. This was very much in keeping with the lifestyles of those whose company he enjoyed.

His last job as an employee was for a Skoda dealership. He decided to leave and set up his own business, selling pre-owned cars by auction. Around this time he was arrested and convicted of winding back the mileage shown on the odometers of cars that he was selling, a practice known as 'clocking'. This may not have been very good for his reputation as a car salesman, and by 1999 his financial affairs were in deep trouble.

That year, as his creditors began to draw ever closer, he applied to Glasgow Sheriff Court for sequestration, or bankruptcy as it is known south of the border, and he was declared bankrupt with debts of £78,684. He was to remain a bankrupt until two weeks before his murder, when the order was discharged. Bankruptcy, however, was only a minor setback for a man determined to become a successful businessman. He vowed to rise once again, like a phoenix from the financial ashes, and in 2000, together with another man, he set up a business called 'The Taxi Centre', which specialised in selling pre-owned vehicles to the private hire taxi industry.

In Glasgow, as in most cities, there are two types of taxi. The first is the 'black cab' or 'Hackney carriage'. These vehicles are famed around the world and both the vehicles and their drivers are strictly licensed. The other type are known in Glasgow as 'private hire taxis'. These vehicles are normally saloon cars or people carriers; they and their drivers also have to be licensed but are only permitted to take fares that have been pre-booked either by telephone or by a customer who appears in person at the offices of the private hire company. It is illegal for private hire drivers to take passengers who hail them on the street.

This section of the taxi industry has not enjoyed good press in recent years. In London, where they are known commonly as minicabs, or sometimes less flatteringly as 'mini-scabs', they have operated with no form of regulation or monitoring until recent times. Numerous widely reported allegations have been made against some drivers of these vehicles, many of indecent assault or rape of female passengers. Some of these reports have resulted in criminal convictions. Recent regulation has done much to address these problems, but in Glasgow, where the drivers and their vehicles have been subjected to licensing regulations for the past 20 years, the industry has often been linked by the media, sometimes speculatively, to drug dealing, money laundering and extortion, rumoured to be carried out by people involved in organised crime.

As a bankrupt, Alex Blue could not legally be a company director, so his share of The Taxi Centre was held and administered on his behalf by a solicitor. Alex featured on the payroll as an employee like the rest of the staff and was paid a wage reputed to be £925 a week. The business was a success. On a good week they would sell up to a hundred cars, and they aimed to make a profit of £1,000 a car. The annual turnover of the company was therefore said to run to millions of pounds. Alex's brother Gavin also worked at The Taxi Centre at the time of the murder. It seemed to be an obvious place to do some research.

The moment I arrived at the company premises at 215 Queensborough Gardens, Hyndland, Glasgow, I saw that the place was a hive of activity. The premises consisted of a two-storey concrete building with the ground floor housing an open-plan office with enough room to display a car for sale, a vehicle workshop containing all the necessary vehicle maintenance equipment, and a sizeable yard at the rear containing many vehicles. The second floor appeared to be more offices and had a large sign advertising a finance company. It sat adjacent to the entrance to Hyndland railway station, on the other side of which was a large dealership selling new Skoda cars, Queensborough Motors. I noticed a man walking from this dealership to The Taxi Centre and back again many times.

I made my way in and was greeted by a young woman who was immaculately dressed and who asked me how she could help. I introduced myself and explained the reason for my visit. I was ushered to a large leather sofa and asked to wait. After a few minutes a suited, rather overweight and bespectacled man in his 50s approached me. He introduced himself as Peter and told me he was the manager of the business. Once I had informed him of the purpose of my visit, he explained to me how all those connected with The Taxi Centre had suffered greatly as a result of Alex's murder. These were sentiments that I readily understood. I had after all spent some time in the preceding months in the company of people who had experienced similar grief. He further explained that lawyers representing the business had understandably advised all employees to have no dealings with the media, and that therefore he could not help me. He added that he hoped somebody would 'be sent to jail very soon' for the crime. I left him my business card, shook his hand, and left. I was disappointed that I had drawn a blank here as I knew that Alex's younger brother was an employee and that the business, together with others, had put up a reward of £25,000 for information that would bring about the arrest of those responsible.

I stood on the road outside some yards away, merely observing and making notes. I decided to take a photograph of The Taxi Centre, and as I was taking my camera from its case another man speedily exited the offices and approached me. He told me that I could not take a photograph of the premises. I wasn't in the mood for conflict, and in any event it wasn't that important to me, so I put my camera away. I noticed that many employees were gathered at the windows.

I decided to take a walk up a well-worn driveway that led to the yard at the rear. I walked beyond the yard and stood and looked around. As I made my way back down this path I had a quick glance into the yard and then carried on back towards the road. I had not gone very far and was some way from the road when I heard a car engine revving loudly. I looked back and saw a white saloon car that I had previously seen in the yard coming at some speed down the path in my direction. I was already towards the edge of this path but I now made sure that I was well out of its way. The car shot past me, reached the road and disappeared. The driver was no doubt unaware of my presence and he may have been very familiar with the route he was taking, but I just felt he was going way too fast given the environment he was driving in.

Prior to my trip to Glasgow in June 2005, I had spent some time unsuccessfully trying to speak to the head of the investigation, Detective Chief Inspector David Swindle of Strathclyde Police. I had eventually managed to enter into some dialogue and had asked him for an interview. He told me, and I well understood this, that he needed to speak to the Crown Office, the authority in Scotland that rules over such issues, and that he would get back to me. When he did he told me that there were issues in this 'live' investigation that prevented me from featuring it in my book. I sent a short and to-the-point communication back, asking under what authority and legislation I could be prevented from inquiring and writing about a crime that was in the public domain. He has since offered to reply to any queries I may have, but he will need to gain authority for any such replies from the Crown Office, and the Procurator Fiscal, who is the equivalent of a crown prosecutor in England and Wales.

After I left The Taxi Centre I decided to visit some of the places that Alex was known to have been to on the night of his murder. Details of his movements had been released by the police.

Monday, 24 June 2002, about 4.30pm. Alex leaves The Taxi Centre. He does not tell anyone there where he is going.
Between 4pm and 7pm. A man believed to be Alex is sighted in Byers Road, in the area of the city known as the West End. He is carrying a briefcase.
7pm. Alex arrives at the Beanscene coffee house in Cresswell Lane, also in the West End.

8pm. He leaves the coffee house.

10pm. He is believed to be in the company of three men in Ashton Lane.

11.30pm. An unidentified man is heard talking to Alex in his home. Around the same time a man is heard leaving.

12.40am (25 June). Paramedics find him fatally wounded.

All the roads mentioned in these movements are in the West End, and are within a few minutes walk of each other. Byers Road is the main and most famous road, while the others run off it. This part of the city is renowned for being cosmopolitan. Coffee shops far outnumber traditional pubs, and many restaurants serving continental food vie for business. Blue was a regular at the Beanscene, which describes itself as a 'coffee and music house'. I walked along the uneven cobbles of Cresswell Lane towards it and noticed the gaudy frontage, which was painted in a shade of orange not dissimilar to that of the boiler suits sported by the detainees of Guantanamo Bay. Pigeons nesting on windowsills above had left their autograph on the frontage, as had a decidedly untalented graffiti artist. Not being a coffee drinker I cannot claim to have frequented this type of place very often, but I settled down with a very palatable hot chocolate and Danish pastry, trying to imagine what the attraction of such a place would be to a second-hand-car dealer.

The clientele present during my visits here were predominantly young and appeared to be students. I noticed some older females sipping coffees while they chatted animatedly with their shopping companions. Large leather sofas were available to those wishing to lounge. No alcohol was served and smoking was not permitted. This may well have been a reason why Alex chose to come here, as he very rarely drank and detested smoking. He was described to me as fastidious when it came to his health and was extremely careful about what he put in his body. He worked out regularly on equipment kept at his home and had received one-to-one tuition in the art of kickboxing by a world-class instructor. He did not pursue this in order to become a competent fighter but as an enjoyable way of keeping fit. No one has described Alex to me as an archetypal hard man.

Once a week emerging musicians perform live at the Beanscene. Little-known solo artists and bands are given the opportunity to showcase their talent, and by way of further support to them the Beanscene chain sells their CDs before and after they have performed. The turnover of staff is high – none of those then employed had worked there for even a year, and therefore no one knew Alex. He was obviously not alone in liking places like the Beanscene; it is now part of a chain of ten such coffee houses in Glasgow.

I walked around the West End for some time, taking in the summer evening atmosphere but failing to find out much more about Alex or his murder. I made the ten-minute walk to Dundonald Road, where Alex lived and died.

The residents of this part of the city, which is a quarter of a mile from the Beanscene and still known as part of the West End, enjoy the fact that they live in an area regarded as desirable and certainly unused to murder. The construction of much of the housing here was financed in the mid-19th century by wealthy traders who had made their money shipping desirable products such as tea and tobacco to the new world. Large sailing vessels constructed in the thriving shipyards situated along the banks of the River Clyde would be able to cross the Atlantic up to two weeks quicker than ships that set off from other ports in more southerly locations. This brought financial reward, as their goods would reach market first, accordingly some Glasgow traders accumulated vast wealth, some of which they redirected into providing quality housing for the expanding city population. Lengthy terraces of four-or five-storey sandstone houses were built, providing spacious townhouse accommodation that was popular among those who occupied the higher echelons of Glasgow's Victorian society. Those even further up the pecking order preferred to live in the more exclusive, large double-fronted three-storey detached houses, such as the one in which Alex lived, although it had been divided into four flats some years ago, like most of the other properties in this area. When built it was given the name 'Bennochy Lodge', but now is just plain old number three.

It looks a little dilapidated these days. Eleven well-worn steps lead to the front door, which has a high arch above it and frosted windows on both sides. Some of the facade of the building is crumbling, and the retaining wall at the front of the garden is mainly covered in moss, as well as being bowed and cracked. Weeds and nettles are the main foliage in the garden, and the driveway to the side of the house where Alex was found injured is a bit unkempt. At the rear, three tumbledown garages provide scant cover for vehicles. Inside, the building is altogether more presentable, with wide staircases and beautiful, large stained-glass windows providing a reminder of its bygone glories.

A two-bedroom flat hereabouts will be advertised with estate agents for around £180,000. In Scotland, property purchasing methods and law differ from those in the rest of the UK. This is also true of much other law, including criminal and civil legislation, which is passed by the Scottish Parliament and not politicians who sit in Westminster. The majority of property is advertised inviting 'offers over' the price shown. It is normal for properties to sell at 25 to 30 per cent higher than the advertised price. Alexander Blue occupied a basement property with an adjoining mews cottage; this type of flat was a rarity and a local estate agent told me that a property of this type could fetch around £400,000.

Many of these flats are occupied by young professionals who have a short commute into the city centre, and others by students who study at the nearby universities of Strathclyde and Glasgow. On average, people occupy a property for around three to four years here before moving on. Only a handful of residents have lived in the area for any length of time, so this neighbourhood is an estate agent's dream, because of this high turnover of ownership. The downside of this for me was that I had to work extremely hard to find anyone who had lived in the area three years previously when Alex was killed.

I did, however, find such a neighbour who told me what he knew. He said, 'I would often see him coming and going in his shiny, blue Porsche. It was always gleaming. He wore very smart suits that looked as though they cost a lot of money. His shoes looked very expensive too. He used to live with a woman but I think they had split up before he was killed. He wasn't neighbourly, didn't speak to me although I am on good terms with some of his neighbours in the house. They didn't particularly like him and this came about as the result of a common cost.'

Residents whose flats have been established through the

dividing up of a larger building have to share costs incurred in the vital maintenance of walls, roofs, guttering and the like; this expenditure is divided among the residents and is known as 'common costs'. Alex's flat developed a damp problem – not an uncommon thing bearing in mind how porous sandstone can be. A survey revealed that the earth around the exterior wall of the basement of the property would have to be excavated and replaced with shingle in order to improve drainage and prevent more dampness getting into the flat. Alex was perfectly entitled to demand his fellow residents contribute to the costs of these works, the evidence of which can be seen today, but his lack of consultation and the manner in which he demanded payment made him unpopular.

The woman who Alex had previously lived with in Dundonald Road was the manager of a French restaurant. Her name was Noura Bekkis. Alex's bankruptcy prevented him from legally owning the flat. The ownership of it was therefore somewhat obscure in the same way as was his part-ownership of The Taxi Centre, and it was put into Bekkis' name while they cohabited. When they broke up, the property was registered in another name. While he lived in the flat it was registered in no less than four different people's names. It was this type of financial arrangement that added complexity to the police murder inquiry, and is still the subject of much speculation among some who knew Alex.

After two years of unsuccessfully searching for his killers, the police admitted that financial matters might lie behind his murder. DCI Swindle told a press conference, 'A financial motive is a strong possibility. This is a line of inquiry we are definitely looking into. As a result we have employed financial experts from the private sector to delve into the business dealings of Alex Blue. We have been working with them for some time, examining his finances and business background. Alex had a very complex financial background.'

Another rumour that had gone around soon after he was killed was that Alex believed that he, together with others, was in the process of purchasing a house in Westbourne Gardens, also in the West End. I have recently been told that this is indeed true. He believed that negotiations were ongoing to buy a five-bedroom house for some £250,000, of which he would own a share. It is further rumoured that somebody was asking for £30,000 in cash. Cast your mind back to the possible sighting of Alex in Byers Road between 4pm and 7pm the night he died. That man had a briefcase with him. No such briefcase has ever been found. A source told me that this man was indeed Alex and that the briefcase probably contained the £30,000. Could the theft of this money form part of a motive for his murder?

I have listened to many rumours in relation to all the cases I have researched, and while I was usually dismissive of such rumours when I was a cop, I now find myself more interested. People often say 'rumour is truth's lubricant'. The police obviously thought there was some substance in this tale of an addition to Alex's expanding portfolio of property as DCI Swindle told the media in June 2004. 'The perceived house transaction by Alex Blue is an important aspect of our inquiries and again I would urge anyone with information regarding this to contact us as it could be relevant to why he was murdered,' he said. 'Over the last two years we have discovered a great deal about Alex, his business ventures, his finances and his lifestyle.

However, I am in no doubt that there are still people out there with crucial information who, for whatever reason, have yet to contact the police.' He then asked those people to contact the incident room.

I made a visit to Dundonald Road late at night. In the darkness I noticed how much cover was available for an attacker or attackers waiting to pounce upon someone. Spaces between parked vehicles, large boundary walls, gate pillars and basements were places where I tucked myself away as late night revellers made their way home oblivious to my presence. Likewise, at the rear of the building there were the ramshackle and unsecured garages and other suitable places to hide while awaiting prey. The assailant may not, however, have had to hide for very long. If there was someone in Alex's flat as was believed at 11.30pm and that person had killed him, he would only have had an hour to wait before pouncing. In any event, what was it that tempted Alex to venture out of his flat at that time of night?

While I was in Glasgow I made numerous telephone calls to journalists and other contacts in an effort to find a source who could take my research substantially forward. In the midst of this I received a call from Peter at The Taxi Centre. He gave me the telephone number of a solicitor, Mr Peter Watson, who he suggested I call. Mr Watson and I eventually spoke. He told me he represented a Mr Greg King.

Gregory Hugh Colin King and Alex Blue had been friends for about fifteen years. King was a qualified lawyer who had obtained a degree in law at the University of Chicago in the USA. He was born on 15 September 1968 and was known by many to be wealthy and to have many business interests. He had a business address in a prestigious part of London and also an

43

address in Glasgow. His father Hugh was a well-known man in Glasgow who had enjoyed a successful career as a bookmaker. King has a cousin Stefan, who is a successful businessman with interests in pubs and property.

Greg King and Alex Blue started The Taxi Centre together. Company records showed it as a 'Private Company Limited By Shares'. In January 2003, the company was listed as having issued one ordinary share with a value of £1. Alex was to inherit his share of the business, which could be held in his own name once his bankruptcy was discharged. As I've already mentioned, this happened only two weeks before his murder. It does not appear that Alex made a will before he died. If he did, no one has been able to find it. Bankruptcy trustees were appointed to administer his estate. They eventually came to sell his share in The Taxi Centre. It was Greg King who purchased it.

It was this purchase that King's solicitor, Mr Watson, wanted to talk to me about. Mr Watson stated that articles had recently appeared in the Scottish editions of two national newspapers in which comment had been made about the price that King had paid for Alex's share. The size of Alex's share is subject to much speculation but has been widely rumoured in the press to have been 77 per cent. Mr Watson felt that these articles could have suggested that King had paid a disproportionately low price given the annual turnover of The Taxi Centre and he also felt that they might have implied that the transaction was in some way irregular. Mr Watson told me that the purchase price had in fact been assessed by an independent and highly reputable firm of valuers, Gerber, Landa and Gee, who had been employed by the trustees of Alex's estate. He went on to say that the value of The Taxi Centre was fixed by them, that this value had been agreed by all parties, and that all was completely in order and I have no reason to doubt this. He added that he was considering taking legal action against both newspapers.

He then asked me what my interest in Mr King was, and I told him about my book. I asked if he could help me with any information regarding Alex's affairs, and he told me he could not. Throughout our conversation Mr Watson was forthright, firm and clear in the delivery of his words. In relation to my book, he said, 'You can write what you like,' but warned me that if I wrote anything remotely libellous about Greg King he would not hesitate to take legal action against me. I have no reason to do so whatsoever.

Alex was eventually buried in August 2002. When he was alive he had spoken of his wish to be cremated but because he had been murdered this was not possible. His body had to be buried in case it was ever necessary to exhume it in the future. The press gathered to report and take pictures of the proceedings. Six men acted as pallbearers. Among them were Stefan King, cousin of Greg, Gordon Murray, who had worked for Alex, and Peter Muss, a director and office manager of The Taxi Centre. Another was Colin Beck, in whose name Alex's home was registered at the time of his death. Alex's younger brother Gavin also carried the coffin. Greg King had suffered from a virus some time before and had been left weakened and unable to shoulder his late friend and business partner to his final place of rest.

It had been rumoured in many circles that Alex's murder was carried out by a gang of criminals to whom he had sold some cars for use as private hire taxis and who owed him money for the cars. It is said that these crooks killed him in order to escape paying for the fleet. I am far from convinced about this. I do not have any reason to suggest that The Taxi Centre is anything other than a reputable business, and so therefore the death of Alex would not equate to the death of the debt. A reputable and successful company would pursue such a huge debt, regardless of the death of a partner, and not write it off. If they did not, this would surely be discovered by the police, and those involved in the business would be subject to very close scrutiny. It would become glaringly obvious that the owners of the business had been frightened off, the debtors would become prime suspects with a readily obvious motive, and I doubt if such a business would survive.

I thought it important that I spoke to those in the private hire taxi industry who might have been customers of Alex. I borrowed a phone book from the reception desk of the hotel at which I was staying and saw there were over a hundred such firms listed in the Glasgow area. I chose a firm that was situated not far from The Taxi Centre, thereby hoping to increase the likelihood of finding a former customer or two.

I got on the subway and soon received a reminder of the inner-city problems from which Glasgow suffers. A poster in my train carriage warned of the dangers of children picking up discarded hypodermic needles previously used by drug addicts, and another advertised the services of Alcoholics Anonymous. On arrival at my destination I made my way from the train to the exit and was a little disconcerted by seeing rat-traps on the floor of the station.

I took a long walk to the private hire firm. Once I got there I noticed that the frontage of the company was blacked out, making it impossible to see in. A sign on the door read 'staff only', so I muttered a curse to myself and decided to telephone the number that was displayed on one of the blacked-out windows.

A cheery and helpful female answered, and after I had given her a short introduction she invited me in. It transpired the 'staff only' sign was to discourage their drivers from cluttering up the office when business was slow. I was shown a seat and was told one of the co-owners would be with me soon. Sure enough he was and he proceeded to give me his version of the industry. His portly figure was coupled with a cheery disposition, and he happily explained to me that his company had been established for many years. He said his was a relatively small firm and that he had about fifty drivers on his books, of whom around twenty would be working at any one time. He charged his drivers £75 a week for the rental of a radio through which they were given instructions about where to pick up passengers.

He told me that he had never met Alex and suggested that I make inquiries at a larger company, one that would purchase a fleet of vehicles in order to rent them to drivers who did not own a suitable car themselves. He said he knew of such a firm.

We then went on to discuss the less-than-favourable reputation that parts of his industry had been saddled with, and he readily admitted that some private hire firms were involved in the laundering of illegally earned money.

This is how such a firm may operate. A criminal organisation selling illegal drugs generates sums of cash, much of which is profit. In order to spend or invest this money freely, without fear of it being confiscated by the authorities, it must be taken out of the black economy and legitimised. This entails passing it through the books of an apparently legally run business.

Businesses whose products or services are paid for predominately with cash are obviously favoured, and this is where private hire taxi firms enter the equation. A taxi firm registers phantom drivers on its books. Each of these non-existent drivers are shown to rent a car and radio, which enables £200 per week of dirty money to be put through the books and instantly legitimised. Five such bogus drivers equates to £1,000 a week of laundered money or £52,000 per year.

Regulation and licensing of drivers can make inventing such a phantom driver difficult, but not impossible. The invention of a false identity is relatively simple for accomplished criminals. The turnover of drivers employed by these firms can be high, but such businesses use this to their advantage by retaining a departed driver's details in their records. They continue to show them to be working, thereby obtaining an identity through which to launder funds.

There are many other methods to launder money, so many that whole books have been dedicated to explaining them. Before I left this jovial man I asked him how his firm had managed to avoid the advances of criminals wishing to launder money through his business, and he told me that the small size of his firm meant he did not generate enough trade for such illegal funds to be disguised in the books. We shook hands and he left. As I gathered my belongings a female employee of the firm said, 'I knew Alex Blue.' She went on to explain how her partner, a taxi driver, had purchased a car for use as a taxi from him. She had gone with her man when he bought the car, and had subsequently got to meet Alex. 'He was six feet tall, always smartly dressed, charming and I thought he was very handsome,' she said. She explained how well he was known in the taxi industry and that he had a good business reputation. She backed up what her boss had said about the taxi firm that he had suggested I visit and confirmed that they had indeed bought many cars from Alex. I thanked her, wished her well and left.

It was a lovely bright, warm and sunny day, so I decided to make the most of the weather and walk the two-mile journey to this other taxi firm. On my way I walked through Queen's Park recreation ground and past the scene of a murder 45 years ago that had a major impact on the Scottish criminal justice system. In 1960, this grassy, wooded area was a meeting place for local gay men. Two men looking for a victim to pick on came across John Cremin. One of these men was 19-year-old Tony Miller. He struck Cremin on the head with a lump of wood, stole his watch and some cash and ran off. Miller was later charged with this murder and convicted. He was sentenced to death. Despite a petition against this punishment that contained no fewer than 30,000 signatures, and even though there was considerable public opposition to capital punishment at the time, on 22 December 1960, Miller was hanged in Barlinnie prison. But the public's view on hanging seems to have had some effect, as Miller went down in history as the last person to be hanged in that notorious jail.

I arrived at the second taxi firm and announced myself. I was let into the building and was able to view the control room, which was plush and well appointed with many computer screens. Controllers worked away, speaking into their headsets, taking orders for taxis and dispatching drivers. When they were not doing this, the staff were laughing and joking with one another. I was shown to a seat in an alcove towards the rear of the building by a man who introduced himself as the manager. He told me that he knew Alex Blue but said that his firm hadn't purchased any vehicles from him. He stated that his company had around two hundred registered drivers on their books and that on a busy night, such as a Friday or Saturday, he could have more than a hundred of them on the road.

Proudly he boasted that his company had expanded over the years because it provided a level of service that people wanted. He said the company had no links to organised crime and was not involved in any form of money laundering, but added that in his business, just like any other, you did get the occasional wrongdoer. I asked him if he knew of any private hire firm that had bought cars from Alex, and he instantly named a firm from another part of Glasgow that he thought might have. I asked him for a taxi to take me to the offices of that firm; he said he would call one, and he escorted me from the premises.

I was soon on my way. It was some miles to this other taxi company and rush-hour traffic meant the journey was slow. My driver and I chatted away in order to kill time, and when we eventually pulled up outside my destination he warned me about the firm I was about to visit.

This firm also appeared to be a large business. A number of offices were situated at the front. I went through a door to an area where customers ordered taxis, and started speaking to one of the taxi drivers who was waiting to pay his weekly rent for his radio – £100. He was getting annoyed that no one had attended to him. After a few minutes a man wearing a casual shirt bearing the company logo and name came to collect the driver's rent, which he paid in cash, and they enjoyed a whispered conversation that resulted in much raucous laughter.

The driver left and the employee of the company turned his attention to me. For what seemed like the umpteenth time that day, I explained myself and asked if anyone would be willing to speak to me.

He asked me to wait while he went and sought advice. I noticed a couple of boxes lying on the floor, one of which was open. I saw that it contained copies of a trade magazine written for the taxi and chauffeur industry, entitled *On Rank*. The front was covered with a full-page advertisement extolling the virtues of a particular type of people carrier being sold by none other than The Taxi Centre. As it was a free magazine, I pocketed a copy. The representative of this firm returned and asked me to go ahead with my questions. I inquired of him if the company had ever purchased cars from Alex Blue and The Taxi Centre. He said they had not. I asked him if he knew Alex and he declined to answer. At this point, he told me that he could not answer any more questions, so I asked for a taxi to take me back to the city centre.

By now I had had enough of going around in ever-decreasing circles, and it seemed that no taxi company was ever going to admit to me that they had purchased cars from Alex. I clambered into the back of the taxi that had been summoned for me and began to thumb through my purloined copy of the trade magazine. Not only did The Taxi Centre dominate the front page with their advert, but they had five further full-page advertisements inside in prime positions towards the front of the magazine. Many different types of vehicle, from top-of-the-range executive saloon cars to somewhat less glamorous nine-seat taxi buses, were offered in these advertisements, under the slogan 'We try harder honestly'.

I later found out that a front-page advert in a single edition of this monthly magazine cost £1,500, and that a full-page advert inside would cost anything from £600 to £1,000. The Taxi Centre must believe that it pays to advertise, and the thousands of pounds that they spend may be a reflection of how the business has continued to thrive despite Alex's death.

My taxi driver was extremely chatty. He delighted in telling me tales of his life as a private hire taxi driver, a job that he had done for the past ten years. I asked him if he or anybody he knew had ever bought a car from Alex Blue, but he said no.

I decided it was time to meet a source, who I will refer to as Tony. He picked me up in his car from outside my hotel. He had obviously done his homework on me because he said he had watched a tape of a television interview that I had done for a cable and satellite channel some years previously. It soon became apparent that he was a considerable authority when it came to crime and criminals in Glasgow. Born and bred in the city, he knew all the legendary crime figures from Glasgow's underworld, and I immediately warmed to him. He pointed out landmarks that had featured in notorious crimes over recent decades, one of which was the Barrowlands dancehall.

In February 1968, 25-year-old Patricia Docker had spent the night dancing at the Barrowlands. At the end of the evening she left the dancehall with a man. The following morning her lifeless body was discovered. She had been raped and strangled. She had been menstruating at the time of her death, and a sanitary towel was found placed under her left armpit.

In August 1969, 32-year-old Jemima McDonald went for a night out at the Barrowlands. She too left with a man, and was also found raped and strangled. The similarities to Docker's murder continued as she too had been menstruating, and had a sanitary towel under her left armpit.

In October 1969, 29-year-old Helen Puttock was found raped and strangled. She had previously been to the Barrowlands, had left with a man, was menstruating, and had a sanitary towel under her left armpit.

A suspect soon emerged who had been seen with all the victims, and who had been overheard quoting passages from the Bible. He had introduced himself as 'John', so the press nicknamed this prime suspect 'Bible John'. These murders remain unsolved, and continue to spark debate in the media from time to time. In 1996, police exhumed the body of a man called John McInnes, who had over the years been regarded by some as a suspect for these murders. He had committed suicide in 1980, aged 41. His DNA was compared to a sample of semen found on the clothing of one of the victims, but it did not match, so he was eliminated as a suspect and his corpse reburied. The search for the serial killer who committed these disturbing deeds more than 25 years ago continues.

Soon after passing the Barrowlands we parked in an area of wasteland that is a known haunt of local prostitutes. This was not perhaps an area that I would have picked for our chat but it was where Tony chose. We talked at length about Alex's murder. We were interrupted by a rather plain-looking lady of the night who offered us a range of services that we politely declined. She asked for a cigarette and Tony gave her a couple. She seemed keen to strike up a conversation, but Tony was keen to get her away from his car. We didn't after all want to be mistaken for potential clients if the police were to drive by.

We discussed my earlier visits to the private hire firms who had all denied buying cars from Alex Blue. He talked about another firm that had a corrupt senior detective who helped them out by warning them of upcoming police inquiries or other activity. Unbeknown to this detective, the firm had covertly filmed him taking an envelope containing £10,000 cash from a rubbish bin as payment for some of his corrupt activities. The villains were keeping the tape of this as a form of insurance policy, should they ever have to call in more favours or fall foul of the law.

He also told me of another private hire firm that had targeted council employees who worked as enforcement officers in the industry. These officers travel around performing spot checks on taxis and private hire cars. One of the things they are looking for is drivers who are working while also claiming state benefits. Criminals had sent photographs to the homes of enforcement officers that showed the officer's children with targets drawn on them. Apparently a whole new team of enforcement officers had to be recruited after this episode.

Tony wished me well and returned me to my hotel. The following day I flew home. Since my return, barely a day has gone by when I have not received more information relating to people who had knowledge of Alex. Much of this I need to research further before I can draw any conclusions, and I was not able to do this before this book went to press. A journalist called me to say that my visit to Glasgow had caused a lot of interest among the local press. Another source said, 'You have got a lot of people rattled. Some are wealthy, powerful and dangerous people. Please be careful, but thank you very much for causing all this interest.' It was 23 June 2005, two days before the third anniversary of Alex's murder. The next day I was asked if I would do an interview via telephone to be broadcast on BBC Radio Scotland. I agreed and went on to speak about my past, about Alex's murder, my research and the book.

Two days later I came out of my house and found my car had been damaged. I went to my local newsagents and noticed a car almost identical to mine parked outside. I noticed it bore badges that identified it as a private hire taxi. I went in to buy my newspaper and was followed in by the driver of this car, a large man who was dressed all in black. He stood close behind me and spoke over my shoulder with a broad Scottish accent. Nobody in the shop knew him. That afternoon someone in my neighbourhood decided to play the bagpipes, very badly I might add, for hours. The sound of bagpipes is an extremely rare thing in south-east London!

These things may be entirely coincidental and perhaps I'm being a little paranoid, but if it is some pathetic effort at intimidation, I suggest they go and find somebody they can frighten. I will continue to welcome any information, I will continue to liaise with journalists and other sources, and I will definitely be making a return visit to Glasgow in the near future. Watch this space.

CHAPTER THREE

THE DEATH OF RILEY

At 4.57am on Thursday, 8 January 2004, a 999 call was made to the ambulance service from a telephone box situated on the B1368, the main road running through Braughing, a small village in Hertfordshire. The female operator spoke first. The line was poor and the operator struggled to hear the male caller clearly. What follows is a transcript of their conversation.

Operator: Hello, caller, (slight pause) hello.
Caller: Hello.
Operator: This is the ambulance service, where are you requesting the ambulance to come to?
Caller: Ambulance to Hollyhock Cottage.
Operator: Holly?
Caller: Hollyhock Cottage.
Operator: Can you spell it for me?
Caller: H-O-L-L-Y...

Operator:	Yeah.
Caller:	C–O–C–K.
Operator:	And what road is it on?
Caller:	It's the Causeway.
Operator:	The Causeway?
Caller:	Correct.
Operator:	And what town?
Caller:	That's Furnix Pelham.
Operator:	Can you spell that for me?
Caller:	F–U–R–N–E–A–U–X…
Operator:	S for sierra?
Caller:	(clears throat) F–U–R–N–E–A–U–X Pelham, P–E–L–H–A–M.
Operator:	Bear with me a moment.
Caller:	That's near Buntingford.

The man then ended the call. An ambulance was dispatched but was unable to find a Hollyhock Cottage.

At about 7am, some two hours after the call, Mrs Josette Swanson, a helper to the elderly, arrived at the small quaint cottage that is Cock House, situated in a road called The Causeway in the village of Furneux Pelham. She was paying her first visit of the day to her client, 83-year-old retired Lieutenant Colonel Robert Workman. She called him 'Riley', which was his middle name, as did virtually everybody else who knew him. She found his lifeless body slumped by his side door, which was ajar. Word of his death soon spread among the residents of the village, several of whom attended offering to help in any way they could. A local doctor made a visit, as did paramedics and the police. Everybody assumed he had died of natural causes, despite the fact that his arms were apparently raised as if in an expression of shock or horror.

Another three hours passed before undertakers arrived to remove the body. When they began to move the corpse they noticed a gunshot wound to his body. This was brought to the attention of the police, and so began a murder inquiry that was to receive huge media attention both at home and abroad.

Furneux Pelham (pronounced locally as Furnix Pelham) is a quiet Hertfordshire village, one of three with the suffix 'Pelham' – the others being Brent Pelham and Stocking Pelham. If lines were drawn on a map linking the Pelhams they would form a triangle. They are about two miles apart and are situated near the Hertfordshire and Essex border, some 30 miles from central London.

This area had been at the epicentre of a crime that had attracted even more media attention than Riley's murder was to generate, albeit 34 years previously. On Monday, 29 December 1969, at St Mary House, 20 Arthur Road, Wimbledon, two inept and bungling criminals kidnapped Mrs Muriel McKay, wife of Alick, an Australian who was a close friend and employee of the media mogul Rupert Murdoch. The kidnappers had mistaken Mrs McKay for Murdoch's then wife Anna, their intended target, but the Murdochs were holidaying in Australia at the time. Before he left, Murdoch had told McKay he could have the temporary use of his Rolls-Royce and chauffeur. When the criminals carried out surveillance on the car, they mistook the McKays and their home for the Murdochs.

The kidnappers were brothers, Arthur and Nizamodeen Hosein, originally from Trinidad but then living at Rooks Farm, Stocking Pelham. It was there that they hatched their deeply flawed plan to kidnap Anna Murdoch and then demand a million-pound ransom from her husband. That was an enormous sum of money back in 1969 and was four times the amount that Murdoch had recently paid to purchase the *Sun* newspaper. Once they had snatched Mrs McKay and realised their mistake, they carried on with their plan to get a million pounds, but now had to attempt to extort it from Alick McKay, who had nowhere near the wealth of his boss. They made a number of telephone demands to Alick, purporting to be members of the mafia and calling themselves 'M3'. They also sent letters that they forced Mrs McKay to write, together with pieces of clothing that she had worn at the time she was taken.

This was the first ever kidnapping in the UK, and the police had little idea how to manage such an investigation. In fact, for many days they remained sceptical that it was genuine. They believed that Mrs McKay might have staged her own disappearance, or that Mr McKay was in some way responsible for her vanishing from home.

When the police eventually became convinced that Mrs McKay had indeed been taken against her will, they made efforts to entice the culprits out into the open using suitcases containing a mixture of genuine money and paper cut and packaged to look like cash. On two such occasions diligent officers noticed a Volvo car near to sites where the ransom money was to be deposited. Checks on this car led them to Rooks Farm, which when searched revealed a wealth of evidence linking the Hoseins to the kidnapping. Mrs McKay however was never found. A theory arose that the Hoseins had shot her, because in early January 1970, just a few days after the kidnap, local residents recalled hearing a single gunshot, and the police found a sawn-off shotgun at Rooks Farm that had been recently fired. It was also believed that they might have fed her body to some pigs that they kept. The Hoseins were later tried for kidnap and murder, and convicted.

Furneux Pelham was established in the 13th century and now has 80 homes and 300 residents. There are no shops, but a primary school, a pub, a church and a village hall form the centrepieces of activity. Detective Superintendent Richard Mann of the Hertfordshire Constabulary was put in charge of the inquiry into Riley Workman's murder, and an arrest quickly followed. This man was later released without charge. .

So there was not to be an early resolution to this case as many hoped. Consequently the media feasted upon every scrap of information they could lay their hands on. Virtually every news outlet carried stories of Riley's murder. Along with the usual array of journalists from the daily and local papers, television crews complete with vans bearing large satellite dishes descended on Furneux Pelham. The village began to resemble the venue for a large annual sporting event, not a peaceful rural retreat. The crews came from as far afield as Scandinavia and camped out for two weeks. Their presence was resented by many of the villagers already traumatised by the killing. The media observed the police going about their business of searching and making house calls.

The press repeatedly used lines like 'a Miss Marple murder mystery' and 'a case worthy of the attention of Inspector Morse'. I despair of journalists who compare real-life murders that leave traumatised relatives, friends and neighbourhoods, to those dreamed up by television dramatists.

Three days after the discovery of Riley's body, on Sunday, 11 January, the congregation at St Mary the Virgin church said a special prayer for their slain neighbour. The Bishop of Hertfordshire, the Right Reverend Christopher Foster, officiated and afterwards said, 'Mr Workman is in all our thoughts and prayers.' The church stands at the end of The Causeway only a hundred metres from the scene of the crime.

The following day police told the media that they had a tape of the 999 call. They also stated that they thought the caller might be the killer, not an unreasonable theory. Consequently the tape was examined by audio experts in an effort to enhance the sound quality, and the police said they would make a decision whether to broadcast it to the public soon. They admitted to being 'baffled', and said they had not established a motive. Detective Superintendent Mann said, 'This is a shocking and disturbing crime. The shotgun is not the weapon of choice for professional assassins, nor is it the favourite of people who commit burglaries.' Burglary was not believed to be a motive, although it was commonly known that Riley possessed a collection of valuable items of silver. These had been documented for insurance purposes and were believed to be worth some £10,000, but they had not been touched. Detective Superintendent Mann continued, 'A lot of local people may have access to shotguns and we are talking to all of those.'

Indeed they did, and licensed shotgun holders who owned them for work or sporting purposes were asked to hand them in for ballistic analysis. This was unlikely to reveal the killer's weapon as he surely would not have been foolish enough to hand the murder weapon to police, but it enabled the investigators to eliminate considerable numbers of local weapons and their owners from the inquiry.

Importantly it was also revealed that neighbours had heard a single gunshot between 8pm and 10pm on the night of 7 January. This was later narrowed down to 8.15pm, and believed to be the time Riley was shot. Hearing gunshots is commonplace in these parts and this one had not caused undue alarm. Those who had heard it assumed it to be a bird-scaring device or someone shooting a fox.

By Wednesday, 14 January, the police were in a position to release the recording of the 999 call, which they now thought had been made some nine hours after the shooting. Voice experts had examined the tape and concluded that the caller was over 50, possibly over 60 years of age, and had not attempted to disguise his voice. The police highlighted a number of points of interest that arose during the call that they hoped might provide some clues to the killer's identity.

The caller asked for the ambulance to attend 'Hollyhock Cottage'. This was the name by which the cottage was known briefly 20 years previously. Riley's late wife Joanna had named it thus after her favourite plant. This was the name still shown for the cottage in the telephone book. However the cottage had been known for the last two decades as 'Cock House'. It was so named after a weather vane featuring a cock had been fixed to the roof.

When the caller was asked to spell the cottage, he spelled it out as 'Hollycock', an incorrect amalgamation of the old and new names.

When first naming the village he used the commonly used

phonetic pronunciation of Furneux, namely Furnix. When he was asked to spell it, though, he spelled it Furneaux, inserting an 'a' that is not in modern use. A sign spelling the village name in the old style, as spelled out by the caller, stands in the village not far from Riley's home.

By now the police had removed in its entirety the telephone box that the 999 call was traced to. On the day Riley was discovered shot they had merely removed the handset, but in order to carry out a detailed forensic examination it was felt more appropriate to examine the whole thing under laboratory conditions. This surely was the most likely source of vital clues.

Also revealed at this time was that in the absence of a known motive, mistaken identity could not be ruled out. A retired district judge, Timothy Workman, who had sat at Bow Street Magistrates Court in London, a court through which many high-profile cases had passed, including terrorist cases, was visited by the murder squad. They warned him of the possibility that he might have been the intended victim, but he appeared unfazed. 'I think this is just one line of inquiry and I think it is not a matter that is causing me undue concern,' he said. He was nonetheless told by police to be vigilant.

The police also wished some of their officers had been more vigilant. The Hertfordshire Constabulary made a public apology for what they described as a 'serious oversight' by the officers first on the scene, who had assumed Riley had died of natural causes. This indeed is serious. The Association of Chief Police Officers (ACPO) publishes a book called the *Murder Investigation Manual*, which lays out quite clearly the action to be taken by the first officers attending the scene of any fatality. It says, 'When attending any death, personnel must consider the five building block principles set out in the ACPO *Murder Investigation Manual*.' These are:

Preserve life
Preserve scene(s) (identify, secure, protect)
Secure evidence
Identify victim(s)
Identify suspect(s)

The manual adds the instruction, 'Remember, think "murder" until the investigation proves otherwise.' Of course, not all the building blocks apply to all cases. Because of the time that had elapsed between the shooting and the discovery of Riley's body, I suspect it was quite clear he was dead, so preserving life would not be applicable. However, the remaining points would appear highly relevant, and the failure of the officers to preserve the scene and thereby secure potential evidence is a breach of the directions laid out in the manual.

The first hour after the discovery of a murder victim is known by detectives as 'the golden hour'. This is because it is often the hour in which the most crucial evidence is found. Because of the 'serious oversight' in this case, no such hour was exploited. The Metropolitan Police now has murder detectives patrolling in vehicles 24 hours a day so that they can attend a murder scene as soon as it is discovered and thereby secure the maximum amount of evidence. In this case the body should have been fully examined by forensic experts as it was found, prior to the undertakers attempting to remove it. It is likely that we will never know what forensic evidence was potentially contaminated, destroyed or removed by the attendance of people who should not have been allowed anywhere near the scene.

Local Conservative MP Oliver Heald, a barrister and the former Shadow Home Affairs Spokesman with responsibilities for police matters, made a statement but did not refer to this 'serious oversight'. He said, 'I have been in contact with Chief Superintendent Andy Wright, who heads up the Eastern Division of Hertfordshire Police, and he has given me a briefing on the case. I understand that residents are being kept fully informed on the inquiry. Such a serious violent crime is always deeply troubling, but I think this is particularly so in a small rural community. I hope that there will be an early and successful conclusion to the investigation.' I would imagine he remains disappointed.

The police adopted a well-used and sometimes useful tactic of stopping every person they saw near to the phone box exactly a week after the 999 call had been made.

In one of the first murder cases I worked on we staked out the scene of a mugging that had resulted in the death of an elderly lady in the same fashion. A youth, who I knew well as a mugger, walked through the estate where the offence had taken place at the time of the mugging, exactly a week later. We found out this was a routine that he followed when going to sign on for state benefits, so we knew he was likely to have been there at the time and place of the offence. This later formed part of a bigger picture that we built up and resulted in his conviction for manslaughter.

In Braughing when the police did this they spoke to about fifty people, but did not disclose publicly if anything useful had been obtained. The same day a meeting was held for local residents in the village hall. Over 200 people turned out to be greeted with the hardly reassuring message from the police that the murderer might be mingling among them as they gathered. In order to assuage their fears they distributed personal attack alarms to whoever wanted them. Forty people took them up on their offer. The tape of the 999 call was played, but nobody could identify the caller. By now police linguists were saying that the caller had an old, rural, east Hertfordshire accent.

Less than three weeks after the murder, it featured on *Crimewatch*. The police disclosed for the first time the type of ammunition used to deliver the fatal shot to Riley's torso. It was a 12-bore shotgun cartridge, which had not been found, filled with 8.4mm shot known as type SG. This is an unusual type of shot, the largest that can be purchased legally, and a cartridge of this type would only contain nine pellets as opposed to the more usual 200–300 found in cartridges used in game or clay pigeon shooting. The effect of shooting someone with such a cartridge is that the nine pellets enter the victim with the force of nine small individual bullets being fired simultaneously. Hence it is virtually impossible to survive being shot at close range in this way. The cartridge also contained a plastic wad manufactured by a company called Gualandi in Bologna, Italy. These wads are commonly found in this sort of ammunition, but the ammunition itself is rare and stocked by relatively few outlets. The nearest such outlet to the scene was in Barnet, north London.

While the 12-bore shotgun is by far the most common type of shotgun, accounting for some 92 per cent of sales, this ammunition is far less common and mainly used for killing deer, hence its common name of 'buckshot'. The police told the audience that landowners or gamekeepers were the most likely users of this type of ammunition, although I now know it is often used by employees of the Forestry Commission.

Photographs of Riley when he was in his 40s, 50s and 60s were also shown. It was hoped this might help people recognise him and come forward with useful information. Detective Superintendent Mann said there had been a good response thus far from members of the public, in particular the residents of Furneux Pelham. He ended the appeal by saying that the murderer was 'determined and deliberate', and had killed a man described as a 'saintly old gentleman'.

And so the investigation continued. Officers flew to Australia to interview Riley's brother, his only close remaining relative, and, bit by bit, details of his past emerged. Riley was born in 1920 and studied at Oxford University, graduating in 1940. He then entered the army and joined the Oxfordshire and Buckinghamshire Light Infantry, which was based in Cowley, Oxford. The regiment had a long and proud history dating back to 1881, and its men had fought in some of the most famous battles in history, including the Battle of the Somme and at Passchendaele during World War I. As Riley was a graduate, he entered as a commissioned officer, second lieutenant. This rank placed him above numerous non-commissioned soldiers.

During World War II, various battalions of his regiment saw action all over Europe, and the Sixth Battalion, in which Riley served, were engaged in the Far East under the command of Field Marshal Sir William Slim. In 1958, the regiment became known as the Royal Green Jackets. In his 25-year army career, Riley climbed four ranks to become a lieutenant colonel, a rank of considerable status with only the likes of colonels, generals and field marshals above him. On retiring from the army in 1965 he chose to retain his rank in his title, as he was entitled to do. Army rules stated at the time that any such use of rank is 'left to the individual's conscience and sense of propriety'.

Then aged 45, he returned to Gloucestershire where he had grown up. He decided to pursue a career as an antiques dealer and bought a shop. In 1968, he married Joanna. She had been married previously and had a daughter, Anna. At some time in the 1970s, Riley and Joanna moved to the USA where they took up employment as a housekeeper and nurse, working together for a variety of wealthy clients including a lawyer and his wife in Dover, Massachusetts. They returned to the UK in 1984, and set up home in Furneux Pelham. Riley continued to work and travel until 1994, when following an operation Joanna became paralysed. Thereafter he devoted his time to caring for her. This he did for nine years until her death in 2003. During this time he became known by his neighbours as quiet, private, and, not surprisingly, a caring man.

On 27 February 2004, Kenneth Workman, Riley's nephew in Australia, made a lengthy statement released through the police, who had codenamed the investigation Operation Sacristy. He spoke of the dread he felt when living on the other side of the world and receiving the call notifying him of his uncle's death. He gave heartfelt thanks to the police for their dedication and spoke of a brief visit he had made to see his uncle not long before he was shot. Finally he appealed to any member of the public who had knowledge of the crime to come forward and help the relatives understand this 'senseless act' and to obtain closure in their loss of a man he described as 'beautiful'.

Two weeks later the police went on record as saying that any shotgun holder who had breached their certificate conditions should still come forward if they had useful information about the ammunition, as their breaches would be 'dealt with sympathetically'. On 19 March, they disclosed that they had arrested a man in his mid-60s, because he had not cooperated with their inquiry. This man had apparently declined to give them a taped sample of his voice, and, as they were unable to eliminate him as being the person who made the 999 call, he was arrested. He was later bailed and not charged.

Nearly six months passed with no breakthrough. The Crimestoppers Trust, a charitable organisation through which people can give information about crime anonymously, offered a £10,000 reward. It was offered with the proviso that the reward would only be paid if the information led to 'the arrest, charge and judicial disposal' of those responsible. By now another officer was leading the hunt, Detective Superintendent Adrian Tapp. He had also worked on the search for Wayne Trotter's killers. Because of Riley's age, the police had a lot of background work to do. Detective Superintendent Tapp said, 'He was 83 years old when he was murdered and so the painstaking task of putting together the jigsaw of his life is understandably complex.' He went on to say that people from as far back as Riley's childhood had been spoken to, but that the police were particularly interested in tracing those who had known him in the years between his return from the USA in 1984 and when he began looking after Joanna permanently in 1994.

Of this ten-year period in Riley's life he said the information they had obtained was 'quite limited'. He also stated that while Riley was well liked and respected in Furneux Pelham, not everybody they had spoken to shared that view. 'He was a military man, and a very successful military man, and he cannot achieve the level he did by being popular all of the time,' he said. In fact, they had examined rumours of tension within the family, between Riley and Anna Mitchell, Joanna's daughter, who had died in 2002. He further revealed that the facts of the case had been presented to a convention of European behavioural profilers in the Netherlands. They had concluded that the motive for the killing could be a deep-seated and long-held grudge.

On the Riley inquiry there were no further police press conferences until December, when a revelation from the police ensured that the case made headlines once again. It was revealed that officers had travelled to Parkhurst high-security prison on the Isle of Wight. What happened there was explained by a spokeswoman: 'Detectives have spoken to a prisoner but, for reasons of confidentiality, we cannot divulge what was said. We can confirm that an active line of inquiry is around the strong suggestion that Colonel Workman was a homosexual. If this was the case then it must have been very difficult for him to cope with during his military career.' Some of the assembled hacks could barely remain in their seats, so keen were they to descend upon the village once again. However their attention was maintained as she continued, 'Clearly this is now the main focus of our investigation. We are trying to find an ex-lover with a grudge. It's the last thing we expected to turn up as he was a career soldier and devoted to his wife.'

It was clear that the police were treating this information as genuine. Great care must be taken, however, when dealing with convicted prisoners who decide to assist police. Their motives must be thoroughly researched and the information corroborated. Assistance is often given because a prisoner wants to create a favourable impression ahead of an upcoming parole board, or he may be seeking a transfer to another prison nearer home and relatives. I'm sure the police would have done this.

I spoke to an old soldier who had served in World War II. He said it would have been very difficult indeed for a soldier to deal with his homosexuality during his career, but that it might have been made easier for an officer. He would not have had to share sleeping accommodation, washhouses and dining facilities with the bulk of soldiers who were non-commissioned.

During World War II homosexuality was still illegal; it was not until 1956 that the Sexual Offences Act, section 12, made sex between two males legal, provided they were consenting, over the age of 21 and conducting themselves in private.

This latest revelation sent the residents of Furneux Pelham into shock once more. They had to suffer media intrusion again and did not appreciate the attention in the run-up to Christmas. Gay media outlets covered the story with interest.

Once the holiday festivities were over, the first anniversary of Riley's murder loomed. A public meeting was held on the evening of 6 January 2005 in the village hall. A new man was at the helm of the inquiry, Detective Chief Inspector Colin Sparrow. When I became aware of the meeting, I asked the police if I could attend, but was informed the media were being asked by residents to stay away, so I did. It was later reported that DCI Sparrow told the audience that 3,500 interviews had been carried out during the inquiry. He distributed CDs with the 999 call on them to every resident, and they were asked to listen to it again. He admitted the inquiry was proving 'difficult'.

Riley's relatives in Australia issued another statement asking people with knowledge of the crime to contact the police.

A few days after this meeting, I made my way to Hertfordshire. From everything I had read and heard about the case thus far, I had a gut feeling that whoever was responsible for this crime did not come from Furneux Pelham. When I was a murder squad cop, a visit to the scene of the crime was compulsory for all the detectives working on the case. This was done at the earliest possible opportunity and was crucial in helping you get a feel for the crime. Reading statements and reports can give you a lot of information about a crime, but nothing matches seeing the scene and its surroundings to give you an insight, not only into the offence, but possibly into the mind of the offender. This cannot always be gleaned from the words on a page. Current methods do not require all investigators to make such a visit, a policy that I think ought to be reconsidered. How can a detective take a thorough and informative statement from a witness describing a location that the detective does not himself know?

I reminded myself to be fluid and lateral in my thinking if need be and thought back to one of my first days as a rookie PC when a wise old sage told me that rule number one of any investigation is 'never assume anything'.

One theory that the police had put forward soon after the event was that Riley might have been shot in a case of mistaken identity. I was not convinced by this. For a start this suggested that the killer did not know Riley and was therefore carrying out the crime on behalf of another. If that were the case, surely the person ordering the 'hit' would have furnished the killer with sufficient information to ensure he got the right Mr

Workman. The killer would not have been told to get the victim's address out of the phonebook. Imagine the potential margin for error if the killer had been told to kill a Mr Smith. I believe Riley was the intended victim, and all that remains is to find out who would want him dead.

This part of Hertfordshire was very different to Borehamwood, where I had been to research the Trotter case. I drove through wide, open spaces, passing miles of farmland and many signs bearing the Hertfordshire logo – a deer. It was ammunition normally used for killing deer that killed Riley.

A main dual carriageway, the A10, led me closer to the villages I was looking for. Two minutes after leaving the A10, a minor road led me to Braughing from where the 999 call had been made. A delightful-looking pub, the Axe and Compasses, beckoned.

I made myself at home on a bar stool and ordered a soft drink, which pained me as there was a great selection of ales on offer, but I knew I had a lot of miles to cover that day. A group of gentlemen were gathered; they looked past retirement age and were obviously enjoying themselves no end. During a break from their raucous laughter I managed to introduce myself. To my surprise, they spoke with London accents. I had expected to hear rural accents in these parts, but in all of my visits to this area only occasionally did I meet anyone who spoke with such an accent.

They of course knew of the Riley case, but not the man. When I asked them what life in Braughing (which I pronounced Braw-hing) was like, they roared with laughter once again. The locals pronounce it 'Braffing', they informed me, so having added to their merriment I took their directions to the site of the now removed phone box and bade them farewell. The barman kindly allowed me to leave my car in the car park, and as I walked out of the pub I met a group of ramblers who were removing their muddy boots before going in for lunch.

I walked for a few minutes to the part of the village known as Green End. Not surprisingly, it is at one end of the village where there is a popular grocery and general store and a few houses. About fifteen metres in front of the store runs the B1368, the main road that passes through this part of Braughing, and upon which no traffic can park. Parking is allowed in front of the shop on a small slip road wide enough only for one vehicle. As a result vehicles have to park with two wheels on a grassed area alongside the slip road in order not to block it. A narrow road, Malting Lane, runs off the B1368.

Just a few metres from these grassed areas is the site where the phone box used to be. Now, a year after its removal, nettles and weeds mark the spot. A number of wooden posts, about a metre high, were put into the grass verge that is in front of the phone box site, to stop people parking, thereby causing potential danger and obstruction. Because of these posts, people using the phone box would park in the same place as if using the shop. To park in any other manner anywhere near this site would make a vehicle extremely noticeable to any road user or pedestrian. I watched a number of people parking this way, and when they had left I examined the grass. Clear tyre tread marks were left. I spent plenty of time here examining every place that a car could park. I also noticed that cars often cut the corner of Malting Lane near to the phone box site thereby driving across a grass verge. At all these places I found clear and distinguishable tyre tread marks, either in grass and mud, or mud and general roadside deposits of fine grit, vegetation and leaf mulch.

I drove up and down the main road a few times, from both directions, and the phone box is clearly visible. The B1368 joins the main A10 soon after Braughing, where from there motorway links are easily accessed.

I drove the three and a half miles from the site of the phone box to Furneux Pelham in about ten minutes. I didn't know the roads and was taking in the scenery along the way. No sooner had I driven into the village than I reached the other end.

I decided to pay a visit to the village pub, the Brewery Tap. My reception from the locals here was in stark contrast to how I had been received elsewhere on my travels. 'No, I don't know anything. I can't help you,' was the general attitude of most, although not all, of the people I spoke to. I wondered if they had had enough of the media and just regarded me as another unwelcome hack. I did manage to strike up a useful conversation with a couple of people, though, one of whom told me of the loud and seemingly violent arguments that were periodically heard erupting in Cock House. The main protagonist in these flare-ups apparently was the late Anna Mitchell, Joanna's daughter. She was described to me as 'a violent, nasty piece of work'.

Riley wasn't a pub man. How many 83-year-olds are? He had only been in the pub once in the months leading up to his death, and that was not for a drink but to buy something from the bar, after which he left. I ate, left, and walked to the nearby village hall. The door was unlocked so I knocked to announce my presence and entered. A small number of villagers, old and young, were gathered. We had a long and pleasant chat, although in order to keep the conversation going I had to do most of the talking. I had to answer numerous questions about what I was doing and what I hoped to achieve. People appeared extremely suspicious of me. They were keen to complain about other less serious local crimes, though. Stories of break-ins to garden sheds and the stealing of gardening equipment abounded, but, when I brought the conversation around to Riley's murder, people would look at each other as if seeking a nod or other sign of approval before speaking. Even then they spoke mainly of their own concerns, one of which was how the reputation of the village had suffered. Their sheds and local property prices were of no concern to me so I left.

I walked back past the pub and then on a couple of hundred metres to The Causeway. On the way I passed the old sign that shows the village name with an 'a' included, as spelled out by the 999 caller. A more recently erected sign at the other end of the village shows the name with the modern and more commonly used spelling.

At the end of The Causeway I saw St Mary the Virgin church. Beneath the spire I noticed two inscriptions, one saying 'Time flies' and the other 'Mind your business'. The word 'own' was removed from it a hundred years ago. I wondered whether the locals had considered having it replaced recently.

I walked a hundred metres down The Causeway, passing only a few picturesque and sometimes thatched houses, before reaching Cock House. In front of and obscuring the front door and windows from the road was a large hedge. I walked past it to see how many other houses were in the road; there were only another three before the road dissected farmland on both sides. The 999 caller had clearly stated 'The Causeway' and the operator had acknowledged it correctly. I thought of how thoroughly the ambulance crew had searched this short road with its small number of dwellings.

Cock House is a modest two-storey cottage with a tiled roof. Such a property in these parts would cost you in the region of £200,000. It is clad with timber that has been painted back and white and has shutters on the windows. It has a front door that Riley seldom used, preferring to accept callers at the side door that leads to a small gravel driveway and a gate. This side door is where he was shot and it is visible from the road and from some houses nearby. There is a very small garden at the rear, and on the roof, standing slightly askew, is the cock vane after which it was named.

A 12-bore shotgun like the one used to kill Riley is usually around four feet long, and weighs between seven and eight pounds. It is not the sort of weapon that can be concealed easily. That is one of the reasons criminals saw off the barrels, so it will fit under a jacket, a raincoat or something similar. An unpleasant consequence of this process is that, when fired, the shot from the cartridge fans out further over a shorter distance than a fully barrelled weapon. This means that when fired in a confined space, say inside a bank, more people are likely to be injured.

Given that the police believe Riley was shot at about 8.15pm, and given the remoteness of Furneux Pelham, I believe the offender travelled in a car that may have been parked close to Cock House. Otherwise he or she would have run the risk of being noticed with the weapon. On both sides of the road near Cock House I noticed many tyre tracks. I wondered if any such evidence had been lost or destroyed at this location, like it might have been at the phone box, due to the delays in finding the body and then realising that he had been shot. Likewise, shoeprints may also have been lost. I noticed I was leaving prints in the mud that was prevalent and would have been there a year earlier. Such evidence can often be crucial.

A tyre track can reveal a lot of information about a vehicle, including make or model. Even if the marks are not of sufficient quality to pinpoint such information, they may reveal if a vehicle was a two- or four-wheel drive, and may indicate the length of chassis. Such marks are normally photographed and cast, although the weight of the casting material, often dental plaster, which reveals minute detail, can sometimes distort an image. Needless to say great care is needed when making such a cast.

Shoeprints can also be invaluable. If a shoeprint is found, the size of a shoe can be determined and this is often a good indicator of a person's height, as is the distance between prints, which reveals how long a person's stride is. A shoeprint may also reveal how a person moved. When a person is walking, running, prowling or standing, different parts of their foot will strike the ground. All of this can be invaluable evidence. Riley's path to his side door was gravel, not the best surface to get clear footprints but very good for revealing footprint indentations. Unfortunately, since so many people were allowed to traipse to his side door I am sure whatever indentations had been left by the offender were destroyed. Even bad footprints can be vital as they often lead to secondary scenes, for example where an offender's car may have been parked, and from there better evidence may be obtained.

Manufacturers maintain databases of both shoe and tyre production as they do with thousands of other products. The information contained on these databases includes brand and size, numbers of them made, dates of production, and often details of the retailers to whom they were supplied.

The 21st-century policeman would do well to bear in mind some words from the fictional detective Sherlock Holmes, who said, 'There is no branch of detective science that is so important and so much neglected as the art of tracing footsteps.'

While I was making my way up and down The Causeway, I was approached by a woman I had seen shortly before in the village hall. I had to admit to thinking that, as she was now on her own and making a beeline for me, I was going to get some useful information. My optimism was soon dashed as I was greeted with, 'You know that cottage has been resold, don't you?' I didn't, but having seen old radiators, piping and other building rubbish outside, the thought had crossed my mind. 'So you'd better not publish any photographs.' We continued to converse about everything and nothing as I followed her back up towards the church. I was still clinging to the hope of a useful snippet or two.

We got to the church and she affixed something to the notice board and then walked towards the large double doors. By now she was telling me about the high percentage of the village population who regularly worshipped, and then into the church we both went. She tinkered about with a couple of things while I took in various plaques and inscriptions, and then before I knew it she was at the door bidding me farewell.

Being left alone in a 13th-century church made me feel a little uncomfortable. I had spent a lot of time in church when I was younger. I used to sing in the choir, sometimes as often as three times a day on particular Sundays. I had even served as an altar boy. Once I joined the police, however, I ceased going to church. I saw too much blood, violence, death and depravity, and took part in far too many un-Christian activities to remain convinced of the presence of a higher being. But I used my time in Furneux Pelham's church to think about my life and about Riley, and I became agitated that a war hero who had fought to gain freedom for the likes of me had been gunned down in the manner that he was. After my few minutes of quiet reflection, I made an entry in the visitors' book, gave a small donation for the church guide that I pocketed, and went on my way.

Most of the villages in this area are surrounded by farmland. There are occasional livery stables and small manufacturing businesses making household and garden furniture, and of course farm buildings. So there are a number of places that someone could 'hole up', should they wish to lie low for a few hours after committing a crime such as Riley's murder. But I think this is a highly risky strategy for anybody seriously wishing to avoid being seen. But let's just imagine the killer and the 999 caller are the same person. Where was he for the nine hours between the shooting and the making of that 999 call? Why bother calling for an ambulance? It only increases the risk of detection, or should do. Apart from tyre tracks and footprints, other evidence may have been left at the phone box.

A field of forensic science that is regarded as being very much in its infancy is the use of ear prints. This type of print was first discovered at the scene of a burglary where an offender had placed his ear to a window in an effort to hear if there was anybody inside the house. Since then such prints have been found on doors and even walls. I think it quite possible the caller may have left such a print on the handset of the phone. The science behind these prints, however, has a long way to go before it can be relied upon in court as much as fingerprints. Fingerprints have arches, ridges, whorls and many other characteristics that make them indisputably unique to an individual, and therefore a powerful evidential tool. The skin on ears has far fewer unique characteristics.

In 1998, Mark Dallagher was convicted of murdering 93-year-old Dorothy Wood in her home in Huddersfield, Yorkshire. She had been killed two years earlier by way of suffocation. His conviction was based upon an ear print found on a window of her home, which a Dutch police inspector, then regarded as the world's best-informed authority at the time, said matched Dallagher's. Dallagher maintained his innocence while serving his life sentence. A subsequent DNA analysis of sweat left in the ear print proved it was not his. He was freed in January 2004, having served nearly seven years for a crime he did not commit.

Fingerprints from the person who made the 999 call or fibres from his clothing may have been left at the phone box. Dirt or gravel fragments from Riley's drive may have become attached to the shoes and clothing of the gunman and may have been deposited in the phone box. Residue from oils on the shotgun, and residue from the detonating charge in the cartridge may also have been found.

Of course the caller, if indeed he was the killer, may have spent the nine hours in between cleaning himself and changing clothes and shoes. He may have worn gloves when making the call, but did he cover his ear so as not to leave deposits on the handset? Was he so knowledgeable and accomplished in forensic science that he ensured not a microscopic piece of evidence would be left in that phone box?

In years gone by, all 'abandoned' calls to the emergency services had to be investigated immediately by the police. This call was clearly 'abandoned', because as soon as the operator asked him to 'bear with me a moment', he ended the call. I suspect he feared the call was being traced and made good his escape, all the more reason to believe he was the killer. In his haste, did he leave some evidence behind? He gave no details as to why the ambulance was required.

Unfortunately, the Hertfordshire and Bedfordshire Ambulance Service did not notify the police, and did not find Riley dead. The police errors we know all about. The errors by staff of both these organisations mean that other people may have used that phone box before its importance was realised and may have inadvertently ruined crucial evidence. 'The golden hour' was well and truly lost.

What if the 999 caller was not the murderer? If this is the case, I believe the likelihood of solving this crime is increased considerably. The caller may have been told of Riley's killing by the gunman. He may have been forced into harbouring the killer for a few hours. Maybe he made the call at the first possible opportunity and is disgusted by what happened but too afraid to come forward. Experience has always taught me that the greater the number of people who know about a crime, the greater the chance of solving it.

I am convinced that Riley's killer knew him. I'm sure a ghost from his past, maybe distant, maybe more recent, came to revisit him and, for a reason that I have not yet established, exacted the ultimate form of retribution upon him.

I made another visit some days later to the area. The myth of idyllic country life was beginning to be dismantled. The people

I spoke to on this occasion seemed more concerned with talking about the new trunk road that had recently been opened and the reducing of journey times that it brought, than with talking about what happened to Riley. Maybe they just wanted to pretend it did not happen.

It was clear to me that not everybody was known to each other in the village, that some people there were rather cocooned and insular. Stories of how people had 'moved out' from the city abounded, and I began to regard this area as commuter countryside, rather than the real thing that I was to experience elsewhere. I returned to the Brewery Tap once again to use their toilets before driving home. As I left, the music playing on the jukebox was by the boy band Westlife, singing, 'We've got a world of our own'. I think the residents of Furneux Pelham probably have, and they can keep it.

CHAPTER FOUR

WHAT GOES AROUND, COMES AROUND

Hayden Hooper and William Banham were two middle-aged men going about their business as security guards. They collected and delivered cash for their employers, Security Express, and they knew the job carried an above-average chance of encountering violence. In 1984, they had been attacked by robbers when they delivered cash to a bank. On that occasion the thieves had been armed with only a baseball bat and Mr Hooper received a whack on his back.

Five largely incident-free years had passed when, on 6 April 1989, they approached Coin Controls, a cash depot in Royton, near Oldham, to make what they thought would be a routine collection. They had no idea of the horror that was soon to be unleashed upon them.

Earlier that day a number of stolen cars had been strategically placed for a rapid getaway by a team of three armed robbers. Mark Mann was tasked as the getaway driver, Stephen Julien was in possession of a shotgun, and Chinadu Iheagwara had armed himself with a two-foot-long razor-sharp machete. They donned balaclavas and gloves and waited for their prey.

As the security van came to a halt Julien unleashed two shots into the driver's door to encourage Hooper and Banham to get out and do as they were told. Julien calmly reloaded while bellowing instructions to the guards. The robbers believed a third guard was in the rear of the van and when told this was not the case they went berserk. Iheagwara brought his machete down on Banham with such force that it sliced through the bone of his lower leg, and left it dangling by a thin strand of flesh. His furious attack continued as he chopped his victim again and again, causing gaping wounds in his arms and upper thigh. Fearing he was about to die, Banham tried to crawl under the van for some sanctuary but was shot in the foot by Julien. Hooper decided to run, hoping the robbers would leave his colleague alone and pursue him instead, but as soon as he turned to flee he too was shot by Julien. The force of the blast to his back knocked him to the ground and broke his pelvis.

Now neither guard was in a position to give the robbers any money even if they had wanted to, and the whole scene was being acted out in front of an audience that had been alerted by the gunshots and screams. A group of children saw these X-rated events unfold from their school playground.

Julien walked around the carnage he and Iheagwara had created, carefully picking up spent shotgun cartridges in order to avoid leaving incriminating evidence, and they escaped. They had not managed to steal a penny. The two seriously wounded guards lay bleeding on the ground.

Police cars and ambulances rushed to the scene, and the severely wounded guards were taken to hospital where they remained guarded by police. A huge inquiry was launched; some of the most experienced detectives in the Greater Manchester Police were drafted in, but even they were horrified by the level of violence that had been used.

Security Express put up a £20,000 reward, one of the largest ever offered at the time, and surgeons, who were unable to save Banham's leg, completed the amputation below the knee that Iheagwara had so crudely and wickedly begun.

Julien called on the services of fellow Manchester criminal Ray Odaha to help him escape to the West Indies, from where his family originated. Iheagwara also went to ground, his whereabouts known only to a few, from where he tried to hatch a plan to avoid punishment for his heinous actions.

This robbery had not been Iheagwara's first. He was an armed robber by trade and had previously robbed many banks, enjoying more success than he achieved during the Coin Controls debacle. In fact, he was known to have netted at least £50,000 on previous jobs, probably much more. He invested his ill-gotten gains in property, did not drink or smoke, worked out regularly, and should have been looking forward to a successful life of crime.

He was one of five children. He had an elder brother Peter, and three sisters. His mother Rita was a strict disciplinarian, and when Iheagwara had shown signs of going off the straight and narrow as a young boy, she had exiled him to Nigeria for ten years, hoping that some African discipline might do him good. Sadly it didn't, so when he returned to the Cheetham Hill area of Manchester as a teenager, he mingled with criminal elements and set off down the path to criminality.

At the age of 15 he met a decent and studious girl of the same age, Karen Sykes. Local legend has it that he saw her for the first time when he was cycling past her. He was so smitten that he could not take his eyes off her and promptly collided with a lamppost. On picking himself up, he regained his composure and walked over to her. He planted a kiss upon her cheek, and so began a relationship that was to endure in some capacity or another for all his life.

Julien spent his time on the run sunbathing on Caribbean beaches. Iheagwara stayed in the Manchester area, sleeping in different friends' houses, moving around under the cover of darkness, and doing his best to avoid the police. Mark Mann, the getaway driver on the failed robbery, was arrested. He began to sing like a canary. He admitted his involvement in the fiasco, told the police everything he knew about his co-robbers' criminal activities, and agreed to give evidence against them. This is known as 'going QE' – the vernacular for giving 'Queen's evidence'. Such behaviour often carries a death sentence from your fellow accused, but Mann knew this was a way to earn a dramatically reduced sentence.

Word of this soon got around, and Iheagwara felt it was only a matter of time before the police caught up with him. He therefore tried to get a defence together for when that day came. Karen Sykes was not the only girl with whom he was having a carnal relationship at this time, but it was her that he approached to form an alibi for him. She was an avid churchgoer, regularly worshipping at the Church of the Seventh Day Adventists. He thought she would be the person most likely to sway a jury. Unfortunately for him, her beliefs were such that she flatly refused to lie on his behalf, and he had to look elsewhere for someone willing to commit perjury in order to save his skin.

Julien meanwhile made a big mistake in between sunbathing sessions. He applied for some immigration papers using a false identity. The local police in the West Indies had not previously been able to extradite him back to the UK, but this gave them the grounds they needed. He was flown back to England wearing shorts and a sun hat, to a reception committee of delighted detectives. They also took much pleasure in telling him that Mark Mann was to give evidence against him.

Iheagwara and Karen Sykes made love the night before he went to his solicitor's office, from where he was going to surrender to police. He was still trying to persuade her to lie on his behalf.

When questioned by two seasoned detectives, Super-intendent Bill Kerr and Inspector George Garden, Iheagwara put forward an alibi that did not require Karen's corroboration, claiming to have been withdrawing cash from another bank at the time of the robbery. This pathetic lie was blown apart and he confessed. This did not, however, signal the end of his attempts to get Karen to lie for him. While on remand in prison awaiting trial she visited him on an almost daily basis, and he desperately pleaded with her to provide an alibi. The seriousness of the charges and the enormity of the sentence he was facing began to dawn on him.

As his trial approached Karen began to receive threats to her life, not from Iheagwara, but from other members of his criminal circle, urging her to provide an alibi. Another Manchester villain with a big reputation in the city's underworld was rumoured to be tasked with killing her as a punishment for her non-compliance.

Tony Johnson, commonly called 'White Tony', was known as a fearless and daring villain. He too specialised in armed robbery and was rumoured to have committed murder at least once before. It was also believed that he had been present at other killings, so when Karen Sykes got the news that he had been employed to shoot her she did not hang around. She knew and liked a young man living in Manchester who had Canadian citizenship. He agreed to return to Canada with her. They soon married and had a child. She would only return to the UK when 'White Tony' was dead, himself felled in a hail of bullets in what was clearly a professional murder.

The trial of Iheagwara, Julien and Mann was eventually set for November 1990. Mann always intended to plead guilty, the other two kept everybody guessing until the last moment when they too entered guilty pleas. Apart from the Royton robbery, they also admitted two others. Judge Rhys Davies described the offences as the most brutal and callous he had come across and gave Julien 22 years. Iheagwara was sentenced to 20 years, and Mann's cooperation with the police was rewarded with the lesser sentence of eight years.

The city of Manchester gained itself an unwelcome reputation during the 1980s and 1990s. Armed criminals wreaked havoc on the streets and murder became commonplace as various criminal factions battled over drug dealing territory and the lucrative business in the ever-expanding nightclub industry. The media revelled in giving the city nicknames such as 'Gunchester', 'Gangchester' and 'Madchester'. I experienced some of this first hand when, in

1995, I travelled undercover to the Moss Side part of the city to negotiate a drug deal. I drove up there with an informant who was going to introduce me to the bad guys. When we arrived we were directed into a shop and shown to an office upstairs. Sitting at a desk was a shaven-headed man who I estimated was in his late 40s.

He told the informant and I to sit down, which we did, and then he produced from inside his jacket a 9mm automatic pistol, which he placed on the desk in front of him with the barrel pointing at me. I told him, 'You can put that thing away. I'm here to do business, not to try and see which one of us is the toughest.' He did not take kindly to being spoken to like that and went off on a rant of which most was indecipherable. I just wanted to get out of there. I didn't fancy putting myself at any further risk just to bring about the downfall of a piece of garbage like this who I thought the local police must be able to sort out. I told him I was going and began to leave. He clearly was not used to people walking out on him so he put his gun away and negotiations began. Huge quantities of cocaine and cannabis were offered to me, but on the proviso that I did a much smaller transaction first to establish my criminal credentials. A trade of one kilo of cannabis and an ounce of cocaine was agreed for the all-in cost of £2,900.

The senior officer I was working for was not entirely thrilled with me spending nearly three grand of his budget on drugs, but he nevertheless agreed. A week later I headed back to Manchester with a colleague and the cash. We were to perform the exchange of cash for drugs at a motorway service station. As we drove in to the car park I became suspicious. I noticed a few strategically placed young men who appeared to take great interest in us. I should have told my sidekick to drive straight out, but I foolishly went against my better judgement and walked to the café where I had arranged to meet Mr Nutcase.

I joined him and another man, whose face was a patchwork of scars, at a table. They both opened their jackets to show me the guns they were carrying. I just wanted to get the trade over and done with and get out of there. No such luck. They insisted on telling me how many of their men they had surrounding the service station, and that they too were all armed and willing to shoot me should I try to steal their drugs. Some bloody chance. I agreed to go and get my money from my car. They said someone would approach me and give me the drugs. The exchange was performed, and for the first and last time in my undercover career I did not hang around to check the drugs. I heaved a sigh of relief as we drove back down the motorway, and after a few miles I did check them. They looked genuine enough but when I examined them closely they were not drugs at all but a dummied-up parcel of dried elephant dung packaged to look like cannabis, and flour-based paste made to resemble cocaine.

This was not going to look good on me, but quite frankly I couldn't give a damn. If I had discovered the dummy parcel at the service station and consequently remonstrated with Mr Nutter and co there would only have been one consequence. That would have been me getting shot. So what if they were all now laughing about having ripped off a soft southern twat for nearly three grand? They could have it as far as I was concerned, but I heeded the warning signs. I had started to go against the instincts that had kept me alive in that field of work for over a decade. It was time to call it a day.

The awarding of the 2002 Commonwealth Games provided a much-needed boost to Manchester. Investment and enthusiasm were abundant, and the law-abiding residents were delighted to have an opportunity to present their city in a favourable light. However, just a few months before the opening ceremony was due to take place, the city was shocked by a weekend of violence that was extreme even for this city.

Two men were shot and wounded in Moss Side. Both were left fighting for their lives in hospital. In another incident a hooded man banged on the window of a house; inside were a young couple and their two-year-old daughter. As her parents approached the window to investigate the noise, the man in the hoody pulled a gun and fired a volley of shots into the house. Both of the adults were hit, miraculously the toddler was not, but she was left deeply traumatised. Still the violence continued. A 21-year-old man was standing outside a nightclub with a friend. Gunmen approached and shot them both, killing the 21-year-old instantly. His friend was left in a critical state.

And on this weekend of extreme violence, another man, who was no stranger to dishing out acts of brutality, was to lose his life. At about 2.30pm on Friday, 15 February, Chinadu Iheagwara was shot dead. He had been released from prison less than four years before, having served nine of the twenty years he was sentenced to.

Surprisingly perhaps, with so many shootings to report, the column inches granted to each case by the local press were fewer than you may expect. Maybe editors thought that saturation coverage of each case might lead readers to become fatigued with long articles repeating similar facts. The senior detective of Greater Manchester Police, Alan Green, spoke of the exceptional circumstances the city had faced that weekend and said, 'The public should be reassured that we will not tolerate such criminal behaviour and we will take action.'

Fifteen months on from the killing of Iheagwara, no person had been charged with his murder, so an inquest was held. The coroner Leonard Gorodkin was told that Iheagwara had gone to the house of a friend, Ray Odaha (the man who had helped Stephen Julien escape to the West Indies after the Royton robbery), for a gathering variously described in the press as 'a peacekeeping meeting' or a 'council of war'.

The inquest heard that a total of seven people were apparently present in the house when Iheagwara and another man began to argue. Iheagwara told the man, 'I'm not frightened; there's nothing you can do to bother me,' upon which this man pulled a gun and promptly shot him. A total of five shots were fired, two of which hit Iheagwara in the head and killed him.

Detective Superintendent Peter Minshall, who was leading the investigation, told the inquest that all the people believed to have been present had been traced and spoken to. This included the man regarded as the chief suspect, but all had declined to answer questions or had denied being present.

Odaha had told police, 'I invited two friends to sort out a domestic and one took out a gun and started to shoot. If I give a statement I'll be shot.' He also released a statement through his solicitor that read, 'I was not involved in the murder. Chinadu was my very close friend. I was standing nearby when it happened and tried to prevent it. I never thought he had a gun and was shocked and horrified. I am fearful of repercussions. He acted cold-bloodedly and could do the same thing to me, or more importantly, my family.'

Understandably, Mr Gorodkin had declined to summon those present at the shooting to the inquest, as their previous refusals to speak would have rendered it a pointless exercise. He returned a verdict of unlawful killing.

On the two-year anniversary of Iheagwara's murder, the police made another public appeal. Detective Superintendent Minshall spoke of 'a wall of silence', an oft-used phrase in cases such as this, and one that is now in danger of becoming a cliché. He said it was time for those who knew what happened to stand up for what is right. He finished with a warning to the killer: 'Murder cases are never closed, and we will continue looking for Chinadu's killer for as long as it takes.'

Today's detectives have a lot of tools available to them that were not in existence when I was catching murderers. Blood-splatter pattern analysis can sometimes pinpoint where a person was standing when a weapon was fired. DNA tests and all the scientific advances related to them have ensured that killers have been caught who in previous decades might have avoided detection. Offender profiling, both psychological and geographical, are relatively new sciences, and the HOLMES computer system (Home Office Large Major Enquiry System) is designed to ensure that no scrap of information is overlooked or ignored.

Of course the police are also subject to more scrutiny than ever. The Police and Criminal Evidence Act 1984 lays down strict rules and guidelines about the way suspects must be treated. This legislation virtually eliminated the practice of 'verballing', which was when officers would attribute false 'confessions' to suspects, who of course would later deny making them. Many people were convicted over the years courtesy of a few 'verbals' and some of the most notable miscarriages of justice in recent times were found to have occurred because of this practice. Consequently, the police have in certain cases found themselves unable to charge people, even when all available intelligence indicates somebody's guilt, and this must be extremely frustrating. But I felt that Iheagwara's killing in a house with a finite number of people present, whose identities were all known, must surely have presented the officers with a solvable case.

I booked into my Manchester hotel, dumped my bags and set off for Bettwood Drive, Crumpsall, Manchester 8, and the scene of the crime. On my journey I passed numerous boarded-up houses and business premises, and many rows of small, redbrick terraced houses. My route to Crumpsall took me through Cheetham Hill, the notoriously rundown area where Iheagwara had chosen to hang around with his criminal pals upon his release from prison in May 1998. He had based himself back in the place he regarded as home. Crumpsall is only a two-minute drive from there and is an area with a large Jewish population. It stands in stark contrast to the obvious degeneration of Cheetham Hill. The houses are larger, smarter and well maintained. I pulled into Bettwood Drive, a small cul-de-sac containing ten substantial detached houses, and began my own house-to-house enquiries.

Ray Odaha lived at 8 Bettwood Drive. It was a large four-bedroom whitewashed house and not the typical scene for an inner-city murder. He had apparently bought the house for about £100,000 some five years earlier. His neighbours' views of him varied dramatically. Some quite liked him and tolerated his frequently erratic behaviour, while others wished he would leave the area permanently and were extremely disapproving of the fact that he arranged a meeting at his house that ended with bullets flying and a man dying. What became abundantly clear was that Ray Odaha was a very well-known man in Manchester. I put my business card through his door with a note asking for him to call me, and left.

I drove back to my hotel in order to leave my car. Sources were telling me to make my way to Cheetham Hill at night and to drink in as many places as I could get into. 'If you play your cards right, people will speak,' said one. I called a taxi from the hotel and the driver looked at me in astonishment when I told him I wanted to go to the roughest pub he knew in Cheetham Hill. I told him the purpose of my visit, but he refused to drive there. The closest he would take me was a large pub near to Strangeways prison. 'Keep yourself safe,' were his parting words to me. I went in the pub and found it even grimmer than his warning had suggested. The filth-stained carpet perfectly matched the furniture.

A mixed group of people was gathered near to the toilets, and on passing them I thought they might be a potential source of information about where else to go to further my research. They wanted to know what I was doing so I told them. With this, a white man in his 40s, who obviously knew about the case, launched into a tirade. 'Listen to me, this is what you need to know: the Pakis import it, the niggers sell it, and anybody with a mountain bike and a mobile phone, they'll deal it, why do you want to write a book about that piece of shit, and put his place in history when all he was, was a violent drug dealing piece of shit?' Some of his drinking companions warned me against going into the heart of Cheetham Hill, telling me that I would encounter 'every sort of shit imaginable'. I'd obviously touched a raw nerve with these people, as now every other word was racist bile, so I thanked them for their help and left. I walked into Cheetham Hill and noticed that some regeneration had taken place but that it consisted of huge warehouse-type superstores. As I stood looking at these a figure emerged from the darkness of a housing estate behind me. It was a man in his 30s who asked me if I was a writer. News travels fast in these parts, I thought. We entered into conversation and he volunteered to take me on a guided tour of the area, provided I had enough cash to buy him some beers.

He was quite obviously streetwise and keen to show me around, so I thought a few pints down his neck might be a reasonable investment. Off we went; he talked virtually non-stop, and our first port of call was an estate called Goldstone Gardens. This was what the locals called 'crack city', and he asked me if I wanted to go to a crack house. I said I would if it was going to further my research into the Iheagwara case. He wasn't sure it would and as I'd seen enough of those in my undercover days I declined his invitation.

Soon after, two teenagers on mountain bikes approached us. They and my guide, who asked that I call him 'John', went just out of earshot. John came back and asked if I wanted any drugs. I said I did not, and thoroughly expected him to ask me to buy him some. Fortunately, he didn't, so we bade farewell to the youths and carried on our way.

We passed massage parlours, shops that sold pre-owned appliances, and I noticed most of the shops had the words 'discount' or 'bargain' in their title. Two solicitors' offices sat almost side-by-side, and John told me that they received a lot of work from locals falling foul of the law. He also laughed out loud when telling me about Cheetham Hill police station, which now opened only on Tuesdays and Thursdays between the hours of 2pm and 4pm. 'That's the only time of the week to get robbed,' he roared. We took a detour around rows and rows of mainly derelict housing. Only a few houses remained occupied, with empty and vandalised properties surrounding them on all sides. A doctors' surgery advertised that it was still open even though all its windows had been smashed and were now boarded up.

We visited various pubs on our travels and I gained a useful insight into how life is in an area where the criminals intimidate the residents more than the police can reassure them. When this is the case, what are you to do when somebody demands 'taxes'? I'm not talking about the demands made upon us all by the Chancellor of the Exchequer, but those placed upon people who run any kind of business, legitimate or otherwise, by those involved in organised crime. To those willing to pay these unofficial dues, and they are often the people whose enterprises are partially or entirely illegal, then these taxes are a way of life. They are a way of buying protection of your interests, which will be supplied by the scariest, toughest, and best armed criminals in your area. Even for those who are less willing it is an unofficial and necessary overhead that must be paid to ensure your business is not persistently burgled, vandalised, boycotted or otherwise rendered incapable of operating. Other methods often involve extreme physical violence being meted out to anybody who will not pay up. If you pay willingly, it is protection, if you pay unwillingly it is extortion. It is Al Capone tactics being carried out on our streets on a daily basis in 21st-century Britain, and I heard many such tales of this in Manchester.

As my guide consumed more beer and became more vocal, he revealed to me his bisexuality and started to walk ever closer to me. I exercised my elbow frequently in order to politely repel him and decided I had had enough of his company for the night. Unbeknown to him, while he was engaged in one of the many conversations he had with people that he met, but who I would not be introduced to, I had a phone number shoved into my pocket from a would-be source who wanted to speak in confidence to me. I declined John's repeated invitation to a nightclub, but paid for the taxi that we shared that dropped him into the city centre.

The next day I was up early and off to research a different case in Lancashire. The notoriety of Cheetham Hill was well known even there, and when I told a police officer of my exploits the previous night he exclaimed, 'And you lived to tell the tale? Don't push your luck.' Later that day I returned to Manchester, and as I sat in a curry house eating alone my phone rang. It was Ray Odaha. He was curious about me, so I explained myself and told him I was keen to have a meeting with him. He had, after all, hosted the 'peacekeeping' meeting and witnessed the shooting. He said he would mull over what I had said and would call me back. Some while later we were to speak again.

On returning home I made contact with the press office of the Greater Manchester Police. They suggested that I send them a list of questions that I wanted to ask Detective Superintendent Minshall. This I duly did. A short while later they telephoned me back. They provided me with a few useful answers, but added that they were unable to answer most of my queries, claiming that it would be prejudicial to their 'ongoing inquiry'. A fair point, perhaps. They did, however, encourage me to come back to them at any time in the future.

I was receiving tremendous assistance from seasoned Manchester journalists, and together with some help from newly developed sources it wasn't long before I was back up north. This time I booked into a hotel way outside the city as my source did not want to run the risk of being seen with me. Clandestine meetings and numerous telephone conversations with this and other sources followed. Information and opinions flowed about serious crime in Manchester and the perpetrators of it. As for the Iheagwara murder, there were some very differing views.

I called Ray Odaha again in an effort to arrange a meeting and, while my call was greeted with an abrupt and unpleasant answer, to his credit he called me back soon after to apologise for his rudeness and to politely explain that he did not want to meet me or talk further with me.

One fact about which there is no dispute is that 'White Tony' Johnson is dead. On 22 February 1991, he was travelling in a white Ford Cosworth car with his friend Tony McKie through Cheetham Hill. As they approached the Penny Black pub they saw another car containing some known criminal associates. They parked and approached them on foot. Instead of the cordial conversation they expected, handguns were pulled on them and they were fired at. McKie managed to escape despite being shot. Johnson was not so lucky and was brought down by three shots. As he lay gasping his last few breaths, one of the gunmen placed a gun to his mouth and delivered the final bullet. Four men were later charged with his murder and stood trial in the summer of 1992. The jury could not agree on their verdicts and a retrial was ordered.

In October that year Iheagwara's former childhood sweetheart Karen Sykes gave birth to a son in Canada. She was now using her married name of Francis. February 1993 saw the second trial of those accused of murdering 'White Tony'. This time they were all acquitted and around this time Karen Francis and her husband divorced. With her would-be assassin dead and gone, she decided to return to Manchester with her son and began corresponding with Iheagwara in prison.

He was to enjoy his first taste of freedom in June 1997 when he was granted home leave. By now he had served a little over seven years of his sentence. Home leave is designed to help prisoners prepare to reintegrate into free society. Iheagwara used this time to mingle with his friends, to enjoy the pleasures of the flesh, and to see his mum, who had stood loyally by him. He would return to prison on time, as he knew any breach of conditions laid down for home leave would delay his eventual release. He served the remainder of his sentence in the same manner as he always had. He kept his nose clean, worked on his fitness with fanatical zeal, and studied business. He was rewarded with early release.

The criminal scene had changed while he had been incarcerated. Armed robbery, which had been his preferred method of accumulating cash, was no longer the best 'earner'. Drug importation and distribution had taken over that role, and a close relative of his had been a prime mover and shaker in this industry. Indeed a career in drugs may have awaited him had this relative not gone to Spain, sampled his own wares with relish, and consequently been in and out of prison ever since.

Fraud was another crime on the rise among the criminals of Cheetham Hill, but for Iheagwara it held no allure. He still yearned for the buzz gained from committing armed robbery, but he decided he ought to refine his tactics; after all, he could not afford another Coin Controls fiasco.

He set about striking up a relationship with an employee of a local bank. Having somebody on the inside has long been favoured by robbers as the best way to gain vital information, but recently criminal teams have taken the recruitment of such people to a much more sophisticated level.

The new tactic that they employ is called 'grooming' and extends beyond mere bank or security company employees. Villains select targets that they believe will be of long-term use to their enterprises. A solicitor, accountant, police officer, government official or other person with access to valuable information, or who occupies a position of influence, will be targeted. Every aspect of that person's life will be examined, and contact will be established with them in a legitimate situation. Friendships or business relationships are established, maintained and developed. This process can often take years and is made easier if the target partakes in some sort of illegal activity or morally questionable behaviour. Regardless, the relationships are developed to a point that when the target is asked to perform some sort of compromising task, they either do so willingly, which is always best for the crooks, or have been manoeuvred and manipulated to such an extent that they cannot say no.

Years of dedicated physical training had given Iheagwara a fine body and, coupled with a disarming smile, gave him attributes many young ladies found attractive. He was a renowned philanderer and used his charms on any female that he believed would help him gain money. He had a saying about these relationships: 'It's not romance; it's finance,' and with this in mind he asked out 'Amanda'. She had worked in a bank for some years, and he felt sure that information gleaned from her would enable him to pull off a heist of considerable proportions. The planning of this crime was hampered considerably when one of the men he planned to do the robbery with was taken ill and died, and Iheagwara's own death came before he could act.

Karen Francis was again featuring large in his life at this time. As an educated woman with an honours degree, she had not pursued a life of crime, as many of her peers from Cheetham Hill had done. On her return to the UK she too had gone to work for a bank and was eventually posted to the collections department. She noticed how the bank went about calling in its debts and decided she could do better on her own. So in 2000 she set up a debt collections company called Quick Release Ltd. Its literature boasts, 'If we can't collect, then nobody can,' and she proudly gave an interview to the *Manchester Evening News*, the city's largest-selling regional newspaper, during which she spoke of her company's skills and expertise.

She made Iheagwara a partner in her business as well as in her bed, and he accompanied her on many calls to debtors' homes. He enjoyed the status of being a company partner and often bragged about it. He was a little less forthcoming about the fact that he also claimed sickness benefit, having convinced the Benefits Agency that nine years in jail had made him mentally unwell.

By night he would often accompany Ray Odaha, who was

also known by the street names 'Mouse' or 'The General', to bars and clubs in order to resolve disputes about the staffing on the doors. Supplying security staff was regarded as the preserve of many well-known 'faces' such as Odaha, and provided considerable income. He was one of the best known and most respected criminals of his era in Manchester, and when he was shot in the arm in August 1994, it was the catalyst for a firearms truce among the criminals of the city that held for a year.

Another form of income for Iheagwara was burglary and kidnapping. Only two weeks before his death, he and others captured a local man who was known to have come into possession of a large sum of money. They took this man to his home and ransacked it, but found only a few hundred pounds in cash. Iheagwara's share of this was £200, which he tucked into his sock. Angry at not finding the large sum they had hoped, they took this man to another flat and tried to extort money from his relatives. They were unprepared for this turn of events and, when their initial demands were not met, they released their victim. Such were the varied methods of Iheagwara obtaining income.

The events that Odaha had described to the inquest as a 'domestic', and that he claimed had led to the murder, were explained to me by a source as follows. Iheagwara lived mainly with his mum Rita and his two nephews. They were the sons of his brother Peter and a woman called Samantha, a prostitute and drug addict who had died some years previously in questionable circumstances. Peter was forever in and out of prison, so the boys lived with their grandmother and uncle. The eldest of the boys, who was about thirteen, had been in company with a woman when they had seen Karen Francis out and about. She knew this boy well through her closeness to Iheagwara and was disappointed by his indifferent attitude towards her. Francis later rang Iheagwara and informed him of his nephew's perceived rudeness, and this led to the boy getting a light slap from his uncle. The boy fled upstairs in tears and made a phone call that set off a series of calls in which the story of Iheagwara assaulting the boy circulated.

One person who this news was rumoured to have reached was Stephen Akinyemi, known to everyone as 'Aki'. He and Iheagwara's brother Peter had been close friends since they were small children. Aki and Peter had grown up to become a pair of snappily dressed young men about town, who turned many a head with their style and charm. Aki had become close to Peter's children, and he kept an eye out for them when their dad was in prison, especially so after their mum died.

Aki was allegedly furious about this 'assault' on the boy, and a series of threatening calls followed between the parties involved. Keen to defuse this rapidly escalating situation, and knowing everybody concerned, Ray Odaha used his position as a renowned negotiator and respected face to arrange for all the parties to meet the following day at his house. Iheagwara was reluctant to meet Aki at this venue, but Odaha was at his most persuasive and reassured him that nobody would do anything untoward in his house, as they would not dare besmirch the reputation of such an influential figure. The time was set for 2pm.

Iheagwara spent the last night of his life with Karen Francis at her flat. In the morning they made love and she has since told people that she wished he had made her pregnant that day.

Later that day, Friday, 15 February 2002, people started to

WHAT GOES AROUND, COMES AROUND

arrive. They were positioning themselves in the argument according to their allegiances. In the neutral and peacekeeping zone were Odaha and two other well-known members of north Manchester's criminal fraternity. Joining Aki on his side of the dispute was a close relative. Iheagwara was given a lift to the meeting by a woman closely associated with Odaha. She did not go into the house and had given him a lift because he had recently injured his knee playing football and was having difficulty walking. James Otache, a friend of Iheagwara, was present to lend him some support. A total of seven people were now gathered in the house.

Almost immediately Iheagwara began to taunt and thereby disrespect Aki and others. He told him he wasn't scared of him. He should have been, because according to the information I have been supplied with, someone produced a handgun and fired a number of shots at Iheagwara. One hit him in the head and he collapsed. The man stood over him and fired another shot into his head. Aki had driven to Odaha's house but could not escape in his car because it was blocked in by other vehicles. He ran. Odaha cradled the dying Iheagwara in his arms and used towels to try to stem the blood flow. Another man called the emergency services and gave them only as much information as he felt they needed to know. He was extremely cautious when dealing with the operator's questions so as not to disclose his own identity or incriminate anyone. By the time the police arrived he had fled, and he spent the next few days holed up in a nearby hotel while a girlfriend cleaned his clothing.

Only Odaha and Iheagwara were left at the scene by the time the ambulance got there. They rushed him to the nearest hospital, but by the time they arrived 34-year-old Chinadu Iheagwara was dead.

Frantic phone calls were made by many people as word of the shooting spread. Two men who had not been present at the murder arrived in a car at Karen Francis's flat. They offered to take her to her lover's bedside. Even though they had not witnessed the events, they did not wish to be captured on the hospital's CCTV cameras, so they dropped her nearby.

Armed police had now flooded Bettwood Drive and the surrounding area and were searching for suspects. Neighbouring houses, gardens, garages and sheds were scoured. Roadblocks were put in place, and the examination of the scene got into full swing. Ray Odaha was taken into custody, questioned at length, but revealed no information regarding the killer's identity. And so began the building of the 'wall of silence'. Over the coming weeks, all those who the police believed to have been present were identified and interviewed, but still the wall stood firm.

Over three years had passed since that day, when I was at another meeting with another source and another scrap of paper with a telephone number on it was passed to me under a table. This bore the telephone number of Aki no less, so soon afterwards I called him. I was keen to get his version of events. I will admit to feeling a little apprehensive as I dialled his number, but his charming telephone manner and willingness to meet left me pleasantly surprised. He was keen to know how I had got his telephone number, but he respected my position as a writer who could not divulge his sources.

I frantically made my travel arrangements, exchanged more polite calls and text messages with Aki and prepared for our meeting, which was to take place in a pub on the outskirts of Bolton. I made sure that I took with me no clues as to the identity of my sources in case I was to be searched or, heaven forbid, subjected to something worse. I wrote the list of questions that I wanted to put to him in a brand new notebook. I deleted any relevant telephone numbers from my mobile phone, together will all records of calls made or received and any messages. I emptied my wallet of receipts and anything except the essentials. I checked and double-checked my pockets and my bag just like I used to before going undercover in my previous life, and nervously set off to catch my train.

As my taxi pulled into the pub car park Aki telephoned me, and following his instructions I looked over and saw him. I fumbled around to find the cash to pay the driver and shoved my receipt in my pocket. He was standing with another man on the far side of the car park, and I walked over. Aki stands six feet tall and is slim and athletic-looking. He was wearing a bright, designer checked shirt, shoes and trousers. His hair is short with small plaits that are dyed blond. He was wearing sunglasses and leaning against a gleaming sports car with the roof down. The number plate bore his name. His companion was white, a touch taller than Aki, and very slim. He wore a black suit and tie and looked every bit a professional businessman. In my black jeans and casual jacket I felt decidedly underdressed.

We all exchanged greetings and shook hands. Aki explained that we were to conduct our conversation in the car park. This was obviously not a subject up for negotiation, so I agreed. I marvelled at the jewellery he was wearing. He had the largest gold chain around his neck that I had ever seen. An enormous medallion hung from it. He also sported a huge gold bracelet encrusted with sparkling diamonds that bore his name and matched an earring that he wore.

His companion was introduced to me as Richard, and I began to explain what my book was about and how I went about my research for it. Aki listened intently and nodded his approval. He told me to go ahead with my questions for him and said that he was happy for this interview to appear in my book, but he reminded me of his right not to reply, should he feel that necessary.

I started by asking him about the story that had emerged at the inquest, that of Iheagwara's chastisement of his nephew and of the escalating row that led to the shooting. Aki was immediately dismissive of this story, describing the whole thing as 'bollocks'. He confirmed that he knew the boy and his parents, Peter Iheagwara and the now deceased Samantha, but that this story was made up and was not the reason he was shot. He continued, 'Chinadu Iheagwara was a silly, ridiculous, unscrupulous person. He ran a 30-strong clan of people, who were involved in kidnapping and taxing.' He also alleged that Iheagwara was on crack at the time of his death. He intimated that these activities were probably the reason why he was murdered. I asked him if he had shot Iheagwara and put to him what I'd been told, that as he lay on the floor, felled by one bullet, someone stood over Iheagwara and fired one more shot into his head to finish the job.

Aki replied, 'It sounds fantastic,' and he laughed, 'but it's not true.' He looked at Richard and laughed again.

He then explained that he was in the Manchester Royal Infirmary at the time, suffering from septicaemia and septic arthritis in his right arm as a result of an infected gunshot wound. He told me that 40 staples had been inserted into the wound, and that he had been on a high dose of medication to fight the infection. He gave me the names of doctors who had apparently treated him. I asked the date he was admitted, but he could not remember. I asked him what ward he had been in, but he said he had been moved around a lot and again could not remember. He added that he had been given high doses of strong medication while in hospital, and this was a reason for his poor memory. He told me that he had been discharged six weeks after the shooting and, having heard that the murder squad wanted to question him, he went to a police station with his solicitor, even though he was still suffering from the side effects of the medication.

I later asked the Greater Manchester Police if they could confirm that Aki was indeed in hospital at the time of Iheagwara's murder, but they declined to answer. I also asked if any toxicology tests had been carried out on Iheagwara's blood that would confirm Aki's story that he was on crack, but again they felt that was another question they could not give a reply to.

Aki went on to tell me that he had been shot on two previous occasions, once in the thigh and once in the stomach. He claimed to have disarmed gunmen on no less than eight other occasions and said that he was proficient in kickboxing and a fearsome fighter, who had fought against groups of men single-handedly and emerged victorious many times. I did not want to put this to the test.

I asked him how he earned his money and he went on to explain that he had interests in four security companies that provided bodyguards and doormen. He said he also bought and sold cars, had interests in bars, and access to five houses. When I asked him if he owned all these properties he declined to answer. He told me of his upbringing in care and of his time as a juvenile offender in borstal and prison for a total of 101 offences. As an adult he has been jailed on two further occasions, once for assault on his daughter, for which he got six months, and once for three years for robbery, an offence that he denies to this day. He has not been inside since 1997 and claims he spends his time building up his business interests in order to provide for himself and his four children.

We spent the remainder of our time together talking about gangsters, who he rubbished as weak individuals who prey on people's fears. We discussed other aspects of his 40 years of life in Manchester, including experiences at the hands of the police, and generally speaking we had a very cordial chat. From time to time he would peer over the top of his sunglasses as if to emphasise a point, and I have to say, if he was a neighbour of mine, I would not choose to upset him.

After a memorable hour in his company, we parted. I was very thirsty by now and went into the pub for a drink. I sat down and decided to call him and thank him for his time. His mobile phone rang out to a message answering service, which began with him introducing himself as 'The A-K'. As in AK47, I wondered.

CHAPTER FIVE

DEATH OF A LADY

On Monday, 10 November 2003, the Devon and Cornwall Constabulary revealed to the press and public that a 74-year-old widow named Joan Roddam had been murdered. Her body had been found two days before in a field adjoining the rear of her isolated bungalow, which was situated on the outskirts of the village of Delabole, north Cornwall. She was discovered wearing her nightie and dressing gown. Her corpse was apparently lying face down, and some effort had been made to conceal it with long grass. A police dog handler had made the grisly find. A search had been launched when concerned friends had been unable to contact Joan. A forensic post-mortem was performed by Home Office pathologist Dr Gyan Fernando at the Royal Cornwall Hospital, which revealed that Joan had died from asphyxiation as a result of suffocation.

The people in this area of north Cornwall until recently had been unused to murder. They enjoyed living in a largely crime-free part of Britain where many did not lock their front doors when they popped out. But only five days before the discovery of Joan's body the area had been shocked by the news that local married couple Graham and Carol Fisher had been beaten and blasted to death with a shotgun at a garage that they owned and ran in Wadebridge, a town only ten miles from Delabole.

Nineteen months before that, 71-year-old farmer Les Bate had been beaten to death in his home in St Kew Highway, a village that sits between Wadebridge and Delabole. His killing is still unsolved and is the subject of the next chapter. All of a sudden this part of the country was getting a reputation for all the wrong reasons, and the locals were feeling decidedly uncomfortable.

Detective Chief Inspector David Dunne was put in charge of the Joan Roddam case. An incident room was set up at Launceston police station. The investigation now got into full swing.

Forensic examination of the field where she was found was carried out first. The location where a body is discovered is known by police as a deposition site. It can often reveal a wealth of evidence and makes a logical starting point. The forensic teams were to move on to her house and garden later. The forensic examination of all the relevant sites took ten days, which illustrates how thorough these examinations are. Quite literally, no stone should be left unturned.

Police roadblocks were put in place near to her bungalow and motorists were questioned. Officers made hundreds of local inquiries and were very aware of the unsettling effect this and the other recent murders were having on the local population. Residents were talking to the press and making their feelings known. The local newspapers were not holding back on their headlines: MURDER VILLAGE LIVING IN FEAR screamed one; VILLAGE GRIPPED BY SENSE OF FOREBODING wrote another.

Chief Superintendent Dave Ellis, a senior officer not involved in the investigation of the murder but head of a body known as the basic command unit, told the media that the police would continue to give an increased level of reassurance to the people of Delabole. 'There is a real concern for the community,' he said. 'This part of the county is very rural, law abiding, and has low levels of crime.' Tanya Bunyard, a local 24-year-old mother of a three-month-old baby, was quoted as saying, 'Like many people, I used to leave my door unlocked but that has all changed. I feel for the elderly people who live here. Everyone is worried because the person who was capable of doing that to an elderly lady is still out there.'

DCI Dunne soon made a public statement: 'At the moment the motive for the murder is not clear. There is no sign that the house had been ransacked and she had no other physical injuries. She has not met a violent death. I think it is realistic to believe that she knew the person who killed her.'

Dunne was keen to interview a woman who had been seen leaving Joan's bungalow a few hours before her body was found. She was believed to be wearing a uniform similar to that worn by a nurse or a vet. A white Peugeot 306 had also been seen parked nearby, it was not specified where, but a lay-by adjoins Joan's garden and is the only place near to her home where someone could park without causing a degree of obstruction to the road. Joan was described in some circles as disabled, so she may have required the attendance of a nurse. She also shared her home with three cats that may have needed a vet. A local paper, the *Western Morning News*, staged a reconstruction using a journalist who posed as the uniformed woman. As a result of this reconstruction this person was soon identified and eliminated from the inquiry.

Meanwhile, on 13 November at Liskeard Magistrates Court, inquests were opened into the killings of both Joan and the Fishers. The coroner for East Cornwall, Dr Emma Carlyon, heard evidence of how and where Joan's body was found, together with evidence of identification. The inquest was then adjourned while the police continued with their inquiries. The court was told that the killings were not linked. This was later confirmed when two men were arrested and charged with the murder of Mr and Mrs Fisher. At the time of writing, the trial has yet to be heard.

A month on, no arrests had been made in connection with Joan's killing. DCI Dunne held another press conference. Some senior police officers see the media as a valuable asset; they utilise every available opportunity to get their appeals out to as wide an audience as possible. Other officers regard the media with considerable suspicion; they think journalists and newspapers have their own hidden agendas and that they will unfairly criticise police at any opportunity. Some officers often develop relationships with individual members of the media who they trust, and it is invariably these journalists to whom information is sometimes leaked, and it is these trusted hacks who get the scoops that their editors crave.

DCI Dunne told the gathered media, 'We are still talking to people and getting information that they think is minimal, although we need to be the judge of that. Our main lines of inquiry are still concentrated on the people who visited Joan, the people who knew her and vehicles seen in the vicinity.' He

MURDER

UPDATE - REWARD

There is now a Crimestoppers reward of up to £10,000 for information leading to the conviction of Wayne Trotter's killers

Local family man, 30-year-old Wayne Trotter, was attacked in Dales Path, on the Farriers estate at around 12.30am on the morning of Thursday 5th December 2002

Wayne was set on fire and later died in hospital after suffering severe burns.

* Do you know who was responsible for the attack?
* Do you have any information that may help police with their investigation?

If so, contact the
incident room on 01707 354236
(All calls will be dealt with in the strictest confidence)
Alternatively contact
Crimestoppers on 0800 555 111
(You do not have to give your name and your call is free)

HERTFORDSHIRE CONSTABULARY

Top: This was the path walked by Wayne Trotter before he was attacked when he reached the lamppost on the left.

Bottom: The path on which Wayne was fatally assaulted.

Inset: The police poster updated with details of the reward.

The driveway where Alex Blue was found.

Top: Tyre tracks in the mud near the phone box in Braughing. These were made at a comparable time of year to that at which the murder took place.

Bottom: A sign showing the archaic spelling of the village name used by the Braughing caller requesting an ambulance.

Top: Chinadu Iheagwara pictured just days before his murder.

Bottom: The conservatory on the side of Joan Roddam's bungalow, which is now no longer occupied by anyone connected to the case.

Top: The step stool at the bottom of the wall to the rear of what was Joan Roddam's bungalow.

Bottom: This used to be a familiar sight – Les Bate enters a pub.

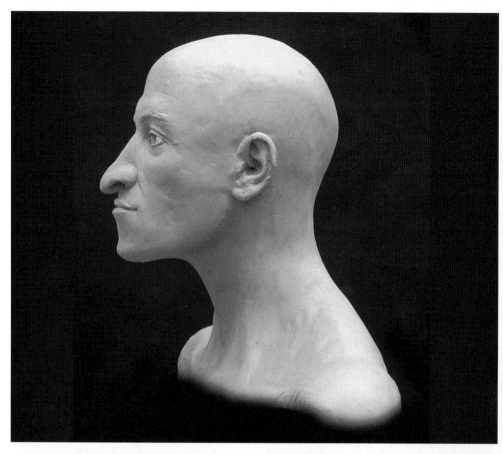

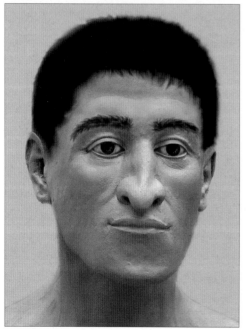

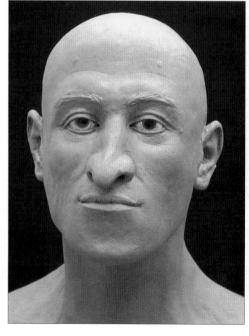

Three images of the unknown murder victim found near Chorley. The modelling was by Dr Caroline Wilkinson of the Unit of Art and Medicine at Manchester University.

On the day of her disappearance, Amanda 'Milly' Dowler and friends caught a train to Walton-on-Thames, visited the Travellers Café and then set off for home separately at about 4pm.

Andre Aylward was shot in May 2001 as he drove back to his Streatham home.

continued, 'We are a month into the inquiry and while we don't have an identified offender we are certainly making inroads.'

He went on to say that the results of the forensic examinations were still pending, and that 38 officers were involved in the inquiry. He said that a motive for the killing was still not established and that a psychological profile of the killer had been prepared. He added, 'My gut feeling is that Joan was probably confident and comfortable with having whoever perpetrated this crime in her home. She didn't answer the door to just anybody. She was most probably comfortable with the offender, which is reflected in the lack of violence used, the lack of a severe struggle and the lack of injuries that she suffered.' He went on to give the telephone numbers of both the incident room and Crimestoppers, the charitable organisation through which people can give information about crime and criminals anonymously.

While Joan's murder received considerable press coverage locally, nationally it hardly registered any interest. Some regional editions of national newspapers mentioned it, but if you did not live in north Cornwall at the time, the chances are that you would not have heard about this crime. It is a sad fact of life that in 21st-century Britain so many murders are committed that a case must have particularly unusual, titillating, salacious, scandalous, brutal or disturbing circumstances to receive national media exposure. A dear old lady suffocated and found in a field does not fit into any of those categories.

Even the local media soon moved on to other stories, but the Delabole residents remained anxious. On Monday, 19 January 2004, there was what appeared to be a breakthrough. Police arrested a 27-year-old man, who was described as coming from north Cornwall. As word of the arrest spread, local people greeted the news with unbridled joy. They thought that the police had got their man after less than three months. Doors could be left unlocked once again and life could return to normal. Unfortunately their joy was short-lived. After being held for just over 24 hours, the man was freed on police bail. The police would not tell the media exactly why he had been arrested but said, 'The arrest is part of an ongoing investigation to find Joan's killer.'

There were to be no police press releases for another three months, but detectives and uniformed officers were still frequent visitors to the area, re-interviewing witnesses to see if they could remember some vital snippet of information. On the six-month anniversary of the killing a fresh press appeal was launched.

Another officer was now in charge of the investigation, Detective Inspector Dee Peake. She said, 'We have had considerable assistance from the community and, together with significant developments from the forensic examination of the scene, we are confident of a positive outcome to inquiries.' An important piece of information was released for the first time. The police said that they now believed Joan was killed in her home and that her body was then taken outside to the field where the crude attempt to conceal it had been made.

The police were now keen to identify a man who they said had first been seen in a shop in the town of Wadebridge on Saturday, 8 November 2003. He was described as resembling the character Phil Mitchell from the television soap opera *EastEnders*. Other people who had been seen in the area of Joan's home or in Delabole near the time of the killing were also sought. Press interest, however, was considerably less than that shown at the time of the murder.

A year on, the killer remained at large. One-year anniversaries of murders are often marked by a renewal of overt police activity, and fresh press interest is often generated as a result. This case was no different. Police officers distributed leaflets to people attending a firework display in nearby Port Gaverne. The previous year this annual event had been held on Saturday, 8 November, the night Joan's body was found. It was thought that the previous year some of those attending the display might have used the B3314, the road on which Joan's bungalow was situated, and therefore have information useful to the murder squad.

This leafleting was coupled with a press conference, and by now there was yet another senior officer leading the inquiry. I have spoken to many officers who investigate murder, and have found that they tend to be divided into two schools of thought when it comes to the changing of the boss of an inquiry. Some believe a change of leader is a good thing if an investigation appears to be proving difficult, as a fresh view may redirect the inquiry or shift emphasis on to other aspects of the investigation. Others prefer continuity.

The third head of this inquiry was Detective Chief Inspector Kevin Harris. He said, 'The inquiry continues to make good progress. This was always going to be a long, methodical, almost old-fashioned investigation, because we are not aided by modern technology. There is no CCTV in Delabole, not that you would expect there to be. This is quite an isolated location and this is completely out of the ordinary.' He added, 'Modern murder investigations are extremely complicated, and inquiries have to be made in a considered manner if the evidence is to remain admissible in court.'

Six specific lines of inquiry remained unresolved and the police

asked for the assistance of the public. No mention was made of
the Phil Mitchell lookalike from six months earlier, so we may
assume that he had been traced, interviewed and eliminated. The
details of the outstanding inquiries were as follows.

On the night of Saturday, 8 November 2003, did anyone in
the Delabole area have any milk removed or used that night?
Was a note left in the morning? Did they still have that note?

At about 7.30am on Tuesday, 28 October 2003, a man was
seen walking along the B3314 towards Joan's bungalow. He was
described as about sixty years old, five-foot six tall, with grey
hair and a beard. He was slim and wearing a light grey suit. He
might have been connected to a small maroon car.

At about 6.30am on the morning of Saturday, 8 November
2003, a man had been seen standing opposite the Atlantic
Garage in Delabole. He was described as between five-foot ten
and six feet tall, and of slim to medium build. He had dark hair
that was cropped at the sides and short on top. He was wearing
a dark thigh-length coat with the collar turned up. He had his
hands in his pockets. Another sighting of a man occurred at
6.45am, nearer to Joan's home. This man was described as five-
foot eight to five-foot nine tall, slim and aged about twenty-
five. He was wearing a black hooded top with long sleeves,
denim jeans and training shoes. The top might have had 'NIKE'
on the front. The police were unsure if these sightings were of
the same man or not.

Another man who the police were interested in was seen
visiting the Spar shop in Delabole between 8am and 9am on the
same day. He was five-foot three to five-foot six tall, medium to
muscular build, and aged about twenty-five. He also was
wearing a hooded top with the hood up and appeared a little

dishevelled. He bought some cans of lager and was said to be 'polite'. He returned to the shop at about noon that day and bought some more lager.

An old style brown car was seen parked in a lay-by that adjoins Joan's garden and is known locally as 'Chippings Lay-by' on the afternoon of the same day. It remained untraced.

A black Ford Escort car was also seen in Chippings Lay-by at both 1.40pm on Thursday, 6 November, and 10.10pm on Friday, 7 November 2003. It had been customised with quad headlamps, body kit, and had a very small front number plate.

DCI Harris emphasised that the police still had 'strong lines of inquiry'. He added, 'We are still relying on the support we are getting from the Forensic Science Service and that will be the case until it is resolved.'

I did not imagine at the start of my research into unsolved murders that I would end up covering four cases in delightful rural locations such as north Cornwall. I expected that most of my trips would be to inner-city deprived neighbourhoods. But my research has shown that murderers strike anywhere, and that living in the country does not necessarily make anyone impervious to the risk of being murdered.

My only previous trip to Cornwall had been in 2001. I travelled with my wife and our new baby, who was only three weeks old, to a place called Rosevine on the southern coast of the county for my sister-in-law's wedding. Some of the guests that I met for the first time were locals and the usual polite question of, 'And what do you do?' naturally followed. When I told them I had recently retired as a detective they were keen to talk to me about an unsolved murder that had occurred locally less than three years before.

On 20 October 1998, a petite 41-year-old housewife, Lyn Bryant, took her dog for a walk in an area called Ruan High Lanes. At 2.40pm her body was found by a holidaymaker in a country lane. She had been stabbed many times in a frenzied attack. At the wedding I spoke to a local vet who had been questioned by police and was understandably somewhat aggrieved that all his knives had been taken away for forensic examination. He told me this as he cradled my new baby in his arms!

Two nights before Lyn's murder, a television drama had been aired entitled *Trial and Retribution II*, written by Lynda La Plante. The programme was based around the hunt for a killer who tortured and mutilated his victims. Detectives were to watch a tape of this programme to see if there were any similarities between the drama and what happened to Lyn.

The police investigation identified a number of people who had been seen in the locality not long before the attack on Lyn. They included a man in his 50s with a full beard who was seen driving a small white van, and a man in his 30s who it was believed had been seen talking to Lyn outside a chapel an hour before her body was found. Detective Superintendent Chris Boarland said publicly, 'It is imperative that we catch this man.' Lyn Bryant's killer is still at large.

As I drove ever closer to Delabole I tuned into a local radio station so that I could be topical in my conversation with those I hoped to meet, and the phone-in on BBC Radio Cornwall was dominated by callers bemoaning the lack of jobs for local people, particularly the young, and the concerns that they were leaving the region in droves because of the lack of opportunities.

I passed Launceston on the A30. This was where the officers

investigating Joan's murder were based. I decided to make a note of how long it took me to get to Delabole from there. It was 25 minutes. I wondered how many working hours were spent by officers travelling to and from the incident room to the scene. I expect that this is a common problem for rural forces, especially for one like the Devon and Cornwall Constabulary, who were investigating four murders simultaneously, all of which had been committed in a relatively small area.

As I made my approach into Delabole I saw huge wind turbines rising hundreds of feet into the sky. They dominated the horizon and looked like something from a science-fiction movie, endlessly turning in an unsynchronised and chaotic fashion, creating I assume much needed environmentally friendly power. They utilise the wind that blows in from the Atlantic Ocean. The weather that the Atlantic brings in makes the climate on this north coast of Cornwall a touch less favourable than that on the south. There the English Channel brings a more forgiving climate. In early March 2005, as I made my way towards Delabole, the sun was shining and the skies were largely cloudless.

I paid a visit to a petrol garage on the north edge of the village and armed myself with a local map. The garage owner pointed out on it where Joan's bungalow was. It was at the opposite end of Delabole. My next port of call was one of only two pubs in the village, the Bettle and Chisel. It was opposite the Spar convenience store that had featured prominently in the police inquiry, so it seemed a reasonable place to start.

I discovered that a bettle is a type of hammer used in quarrying and shaping slate. The people of Delabole pride themselves on the fact that their village is a working village, and unlike many others in the surrounding area its main source of income is not obtained from tourism. Many of the men work in the building trade, both locally and wherever work may take them. Some people work in the few local businesses that exist: small shops and manufacturing, or in the slate quarry, which has a proud 600-year heritage. Only about forty or so people work there now, as opposed to many hundreds in bygone years. Delabole slate is beautiful. I saw many fine examples of it: tiles, tables, work surfaces, and any listed building in the area that has used such slate in its construction must have subsequent work repairs carried out using only original Delabole slate. The downsizing of the quarry work over the years could have meant the death of this village as the railway station, the hotels, the cinema and other quarry-related businesses disappeared. But to the resolute and adaptable people of Delabole it meant a challenge that had to be faced, and it is testament to their abilities that the village survives today.

The village housing consists mainly of small cottages, some bungalows and some larger detached properties that are found towards the outskirts of town. There has been a recent housing development constructed to accommodate people moving to the area. One of the attractions of Delabole is that property prices are less than in some neighbouring areas. Locals told me this was because it was known as a living, breathing, working community village, not a more glamorous area where comfortably off retired folk set up home. Neither does it have a proliferation of holiday home accommodation. Delabole boasts a working men's club, the only one I saw during my extensive travels around these parts.

I moved on to Joan's bungalow, which is called West Brow. I

wanted to see it before it got dark. As I travelled south out of the village I noticed how houses became fewer and fewer until they appeared only occasionally. A mile and a half from the village centre on the right I saw West Brow, a small whitewashed single-storey bungalow. If you blinked when driving past you would miss it; it is that unobtrusive. I drove past, as I wanted to see if it was any more noticeable when heading north along the B3314.

I turned my car around in the next village, Westdowns, and headed back. The wind turbines once again dominated the horizon from this approach. When I was 200 metres from West Brow, I could see its chimney and roof. I was, of course, looking for such features because I knew the bungalow was there. If you did not, the most likely scenario is that you would pass it without noticing, especially in the dark.

I parked in the lay-by that adjoins the garden of West Brow and has been mentioned earlier as 'Chippings Lay-by'. It is about fifty metres long and nine metres wide and big enough to accommodate most vehicles on our roads today, including cars towing caravans, which frequently use it in the summer months. Lay-bys of this size are a rarity in these parts.

West Brow somewhat unusually has no back garden but has gardens to the front and on both sides. These stand neglected; a large pond lies stagnant, a pile of rubble appears to have been fly-tipped there, and I noticed the remnants of a bonfire. A slate wall, which is home to wild grasses and weeds, runs around the borders of the property.

A front gate opens on to a short path that leads to the front door. Inside the gate I noticed a six-pint milk bottle holder. Above the front door is a light, the type with a sensor that illuminates when anything passes. This was in place at the time of Joan's murder. Two CCTV cameras have been installed since the murder. One is mounted above the front door and points in the direction of the front gate. The other is fixed to the front wall and faces in the direction of Chippings Lay-by. I would imagine these were installed to deter would-be burglars, as the property has been unoccupied since Joan's murder. They may have been installed by the police in an effort to capture on film any offender returning to the scene of the crime. If I was presiding over any such installation, I would have concealed high-tech miniature cameras that were invisible to the naked eye.

Certain criminals, including murderers, often return to the scenes of their wrongdoing. In the Lyn Bryant case it was believed the offender did just that, returning some days later to place a pair of spectacles at the scene in an apparent effort to taunt those trying to catch him. Arsonists in particular are known to do this. They enjoy seeing the results of their handiwork, and like to observe the fire services battling blazes.

One such arsonist I dealt with in my time in the police was captured when we quickly deployed plain-clothes officers into the areas near to where he set his fires. The premises he chose were usually large retail stores or warehouses, and as soon as we were notified of such a fire by the fire service, vantage points from which it was possible to view the blaze would be identified and observed. These deliberate fires only happened during the winter months. This extremely dangerous individual was caught when officers saw him gazing at one such fire, with his hands in the pockets of his full-length overcoat. When the officers searched him they found he had removed the insides of his coat pockets in order that he could undo his trouser flies and pleasure himself while watching the fires. He did not commit these offences in the warmer months, as he felt wearing an overcoat would look too suspicious.

Back at West Brow I must admit to being slightly concerned when I saw the CCTV cameras. I wondered if my image had been captured on them and if the local constabulary were screeching through country lanes on their way to apprehend me. Over the years the bungalow had been extended. A bedroom had been added on one side and a conservatory on the other. The elements had taken their toll on the property. Wind and rain sweeps in from the Atlantic Ocean during the winter months and locals told me that failure to maintain a property regularly can result in irreparable damage. This bungalow was no exception.

Beyond the rear wall of West Brow there is an 18-inch gap and then a slate wall. This wall borders the field in which Joan's body was found. The wall is about four feet high and about one foot wide. Propped against this wall I saw a step stool consisting of two plastic steps in a tubular metal frame. I was puzzled as to why it was there. This section of wall appeared to me to be the most likely place at which Joan's body was taken into the field. It was clear of rubbish and undergrowth, which in all other places made access to the wall, and thereby the field, difficult. So who had put the steps there? If they had been in place at the time her body was found, they should have been taken away for vital forensic examination. If the police had put them there in order to make climbing over the wall easier, they should definitely have been removed when they had finished with the scene.

It is becoming increasingly common for juries in criminal trials to ask to visit the scene of a crime. All parties involved in a trial attend, and sharp-eyed barristers are forever looking for something to turn to their client's advantage. If this case ever results in a trial and a visit to the scene, a barrister may well ask the police the same question that entered my head – 'Who put those there?' If the police had left them there by mistake and had to admit to that, a barrister would seek to exploit this by undermining the thoroughness of police actions. There may of course be some other explanation as to why the steps were there, but nevertheless it was a strange find.

Having seen the bungalow in daylight, I left to try to find out more about Joan. I wanted to see if I could make some sense of this baffling crime. Joan and her husband Frank moved to Cornwall when she retired. Nobody could be precise as to when this was, but it was thought to be about fifteen years before her death. Joan had previously worked as a dressmaker; she did not have any children but had nephews and nieces who she spoke of in glowing terms, and whose visits were always reason for much excitement. Locals believed that she had relations living in Essex. Those who knew Joan and Frank described them as being well liked. They were referred to as coming from 'up country', a Cornish term for anybody who comes from east of the county, but they had apparently settled easily into the Cornish way of life. Frank had retired from the Navy and worked as a chef in a nearby pub. He died six years before Joan, and thereafter she lived alone in West Brow with her cats. After her murder the cats were re-housed by a couple who lived nearby.

Joan was five-foot four tall, of slender build, and she took great pride in her appearance whenever she ventured out. Her clothing was always immaculate and described as being 'most appropriate' for a lady of her age. Joan had her hair attended to each week, a wash and blow-dry, but every six weeks she would also have the colour re-tinted. And very particular about it she was too. Not for her one preferred tone but a combination of three colours: three quarters sirocco, a touch of very light blonde, and a further touch of very light golden blonde. When it came to her personal grooming, there could be no compromise. Her trips to the hairdressers were on a Wednesday when she also did her weekly shop at the local Spar.

As she did not drive, her trusted local taxi driver would be on hand each week to do the round trip. Her shopping was always paid for by credit or debit card, never cash, and she was further described as being polite and courteous. These weekly trips were a social event for her as she would spend time talking to the people she regularly met. Joan would not indulge in the gossip and rumour of the village, but she would gladly talk about any other subject that arose. She always purchased large amounts of cat food, and sometimes she would buy a bottle of sherry as she enjoyed the occasional glass.

Joan was not widely known in the village as she led in essence a quiet life. But to the people she did know she brought joy whenever they met. I now had a clear picture of the lady, so I decided to concentrate on the outstanding inquiries that the police had asked the public to assist with in November 2004.

I discovered that a vagrant had been seen in and around the village around the time of Joan's murder. He must have been a hardy character as he was often seen sleeping in gardens and hedgerows in November. He would often steal a pint of milk from doorsteps for his breakfast, and would sometimes leave a note apologising for these crimes. I believe he remains untraced and it would appear he has moved on, as he has not been sighted recently.

The grey-haired, slim 60-year-old man who possibly had a maroon car did not sound familiar to the locals I spoke to. The police had previously disclosed that Joan was murdered in her home and then taken to the field. Joan was slim and probably around eight stone in weight. To transport her lifeless body from the house, around the garden and then up and over the wall requires a considerable degree of strength for somebody acting alone. This was all done without causing further injury to her body – quite remarkable as the stone wall had many sharp edges that could easily have caused damage to her corpse. Two offenders would have been able to carry and place her over the wall more easily, but most murders like this one are committed by people acting alone. If Joan was killed by a lone offender, he must have had the necessary physical attributes, and I don't believe a slim 60-year-old man would have been capable of doing this without dragging or pulling the corpse over the wall, thereby causing damage to it.

Furthermore, if this man was the killer, and if he was driving the maroon car, I think he would have put the body in the boot of his car and disposed of it elsewhere.

One of the most common factors that witnesses often get wrong is a person's height. Try judging a person's height if they are standing and you are sitting. It is especially difficult to do when sitting in a car, where a sighting may last for a very short space of time. It is still not an easy thing to do when standing unless you are positioned very close to someone. Add to that the fact that many people have inaccurate perceptions of their own height, and you can see why this is often a very imprecise factor in descriptions given to police.

This is part of the reason that I believe the two persons referred to in the sightings near the Delabole garage could be the same person. Two of the descriptions state he was wearing a hooded top. The other says a collar was turned up and this may have been confused with a hooded top. The ages given are the same – 25 years old. If I am right, I think it unlikely that this person was the killer. I have established that he purchased 12 large cans of Stella Artois lager on his first visit to the Spar shop, and another dozen on his return some three hours later. Stella Artois is a stronger than average lager, and this may well indicate that he was not drinking alone. The police stated that he might have attended a party on the night of Friday, 7 November. I've heard that this man was in a jovial mood on the morning of Saturday, 8 November, despite being bothered by quite a nasty cut on his hand. He was reluctant to explain how he came by this other than to indicate it was as a result of high jinks. This man did not speak with a local accent and was believed to come from 'up country'. A source went on to explain that this man also appeared to have been smoking cannabis. If he had already killed Joan, I very much doubt he would have stayed in the village drinking lager. If he was to kill her later, would he do so with a cut on his hand that had been clearly seen by witnesses, and which could leave incriminating blood evidence at the scene? I suspect not.

The customised car sounded to me like it would belong to a younger person, so I made myself busy with some of the local car-driving youths in an effort to find out what I could.

Nobody recognised its description, nor could they provide me with any other clues as to its ownership or whereabouts.

I decided to revisit West Brow at night. It is quite possible that this offence took place in the dark. If this had been the case I agree with the police that the culprit must have known Joan, as we know she did not open her door to strangers. The light by her front door would have illuminated any caller. The dark would have provided some cover when moving the body, but I am puzzled as to why the culprit did this. It appears to me to have been an unnecessary thing to do, something that would not only have increased the risk of being seen but also the chances of leaving incriminating forensic evidence.

This stems from the science that backs up the well-known saying among forensic scientists: 'every contact leaves a trace'. All fabrics, whether they are natural or synthetic, shed fibres. This applies not only to clothing, but equally to upholstery, blankets, carpets and so on. Fibres may transfer either way: from a victim's clothing to the offender's, or in the opposite direction. In this instance, Joan's night attire would become the starting point for a forensic examiner attempting to obtain such evidence. There are a number of ways in which an examiner can retrieve this sort of evidence. Fibres visible to the naked eye can be lifted using tweezers. In the absence of visible evidence, an item of clothing or other piece of material can be vacuumed using specially designed vacuum machines. These have filters fitted to them in order to catch fibres and other particles and are many times more powerful than a domestic vacuum cleaner. It is vital that a new filter is used on each examination in order not to cross-contaminate any potential evidence.

Lifting tape may also be used for this purpose, although this is not a popular method among some forensic examiners. Static electricity lifting devices have also recently been developed, and the advantage of these is that they do not need an adhesive to perform the lift, which lifting tape does.

Once any fibres have been retrieved they are examined under laboratory conditions. A microscope is used to determine the type of fibre. This examination can determine if it is cotton, wool or synthetic. It may also be examined by cross-section. This is useful for man-made fibres such as nylon, as they begin their life as liquids and during manufacture they are pushed through a nozzle of some description. These nozzles vary in shape; some are round, others square or oval. Determining the cross-sectional shape and width of a fibre can sometimes help in establishing the type and source of material from where it originated. A fibre will also be examined to see if it contains any chemicals that have been added by manufacturers to control the sheen and brightness of the material.

A microspectrophotometry test can also be carried out. This sends beams of light through the fibre to establish its colour according to how much light passes through. If the fibre is large enough for the colour to be physically extracted by slicing a section of it, a chromatography test can be done to find out which dyes were used in its manufacture. This again is useful in finding out the original source of the material. When dealing with man-made fibres there is yet another test, called a spectrophotometry test, which can be done using chemicals to find out what type of synthetic a fibre has come from – say nylon, polyester or acrylic.

One of the most famous recent cases in which evidence of fibres proved vital was the murder of eight-year-old Sarah Payne in 2000. A 17-month forensic examination was carried out during which many fibres were retrieved and painstakingly examined. A fibre found in some of the hair remaining on her decomposing body was shown to have come from the upholstery of a van belonging to a suspect who the police had chosen to look closely at – Roy Whiting. Other fibres found in a Velcro strap on one of her shoes that was recovered were proved to match those of a red sweatshirt found in Whiting's van. This evidence contributed significantly to his conviction for kidnap and murder.

As British manufacturing declines, more retailers are sourcing clothing from countries like China and Indonesia. I hope these emerging economies keep stringent records of the manufacture of fabrics used in their clothing, in order that fibres found at crime scenes can continue to be traced.

The partial covering of Joan's body with long grass puzzles me. It can hardly be considered to be a concerted effort to ensure her body would never be found. I wonder if the body was taken out of the house to prevent the cats from devouring it, as they would have done this when they began to starve. I prefer to think that the killer did this in an effort to buy himself some time. If he had left Joan's body in the house, the chances are it would have been discovered earlier. This would have reduced the time the offender had to get away. A local offender would also wish to buy himself some time in order to dispose of his clothing and any other incriminating evidence.

The police revealed that her body was lying face down and I wonder whether this was significant. Could the culprit have begun to realise the enormity of this crime, and therefore not been able to confront her lifeless face?

A vital tool for the police in capturing offenders is psychological profiling. Experts draw up a profile of the type of person they believe would have committed a particular crime. Such an expert was called in to assist this inquiry.

Some of the earliest work in this field of science was carried out by the Behavioural Science Unit (BSU) of the FBI. The BSU is the unit made famous in the film *The Silence of the Lambs*, starring Anthony Hopkins as the crazed serial killer and cannibal Hannibal Lecter, and Jodie Foster as the agent Clarice Starling, who was tasked with exploring his deranged mind. Many years ago the BSU began to classify murderers into two categories – 'organised' and 'disorganised'.

The profile characteristics of the organised and disorganised murderer are described as follows.

ORGANISED MURDERER	DISORGANISED MURDERER
Average to above average intelligence	Below average intelligence
Socially competent	Socially inadequate
Prefers skilled work	Has an unskilled job
Sexually competent	Sexually incompetent
High in family birth order	Low in family birth order
Father has stable job	Father's work unstable
Inconsistent childhood discipline	Harsh discipline as a child
Controls his mood during crime	Anxious mood during crime
Use of alcohol with crime	Minimal use of alcohol
Precipitating situational stress	Minimal situational stress
Lives with a partner	Lives alone
Uses a well-maintained car	Lives or works near to crime scene
Follows his crime in the media	Minimal interest in news media
May change jobs or move to different area after crime	Significant behaviour change; may turn to drugs, alcohol or religion

Details of a crime and crime–scene features are also categorised by the BSU according to whether the perpetrator is organised or disorganised.

ORGANISED MURDERER	DISORGANISED MURDERER
Planned offence	Spontaneous offence
Victim was a targeted stranger	Victim or location known
Personalises victim	Depersonalises victim
Controlled conversation	Minimal conversation
Crime scene reflects overall control	Crime scene random and sloppy
Demands a submissive victim	Sudden violence towards victim
Restraints used	Minimal use of restraints
Aggressive acts prior to death	Sexual acts after death
Body hidden	Body left in view
Weapon or evidence absent	Evidence or weapon often present
Transports victim or body	Body left at death scene

This second table is sometimes used by investigators when trying to pinpoint the type of person they believe to be responsible for a particular crime. I decided to do the same with Joan's murder. I took what we knew about the crime and the scene, added my own opinions, and then saw which boxes I ticked. I believe eight of the eleven characteristics of an organised murderer are applicable.

Firstly, I think this offence was planned. The remoteness of Joan's cottage makes a random attack unlikely. No effort was made to depersonalise Joan. She was not mutilated or disfigured in any way. I believe controlled conversation must have taken place in order for the offender to gain access to her home. The crime scene showed overall control of Joan by the offender.

There was no evidence of theft or ransacking. A lack of injuries to her body indicates submissiveness. The body was hidden. No obvious evidence was found. The police would most likely have disclosed any. Joan's body was transported into the field.

I have not been able to compare any possible suspect's profile with the characteristics of an organised murderer, because there is no such suspect. Perhaps you may be able to if there is someone you feel could have been responsible for this crime. All contributions gratefully received.

CHAPTER SIX

AN ENGLISHMAN'S HOME

Millionaire, tough, outgoing, opinionated, rogue – these are just a few of the words used to describe 71-year-old Cornish farmer Les Bate, who was last seen alive leaving the Maltsters Arms public house in the tiny Cornish village of Chapel Amble at about 11.30pm on Friday, 12 April 2002.

Les enjoyed a drink most nights. Lager was his preferred beverage and he would sink a few pints, enjoy a chat with some of the locals, and tell a joke or two, before climbing into his Land Rover to make the short journey home. This night was no different. There had been about thirty people drinking in the pub, but many of them had felt the need to warn Les about flashing his money about. One friend went so far as to tell him that he was being watched by some customers who were unknown to the locals. Les was indisputably wealthy and always liked to have plenty of cash on him, but this night he was particularly open about the fact that in his tan-coloured wallet he had a cheque for £11,000 and about £1,000 in cash.

He made the short journey home along some narrow country lanes before reaching the A39, a main road that the locals call 'The Atlantic Highway'. He turned left and drove a short way to his detached farmhouse, Tregilders Farm. The distance from the pub to his home is less than two miles, he knew the roads like the back of his hand, and on arriving home he parked in his usual place, a drive at the side of his house.

Following a burglary at his home the previous October, Les had started to take what he thought were reasonable precautions. He never entered his house through the front door, preferring to use a door at the back that led to a utility room.

Les was a widower and lived alone. His beloved but long-suffering wife Nancy had died two years previously from cancer. He had two children: a daughter, Kathy Arnold, who lived in Melbourne, Australia, and a son, Martin, who lived locally. That weekend in April, Kathy tried phoning her dad but could get no answer. She contacted Martin who went to the house at about 11.30am on the Sunday morning. He found his father inside the house lying dead in a pool of blood close to the back door. He raised the alarm and the police attended.

At first it was thought that he might have died as a result of a fall; there was no evidence of a burglary and no obvious weapon present. In any event, this village had not had a violent crime reported since 1373! A post-mortem was carried out, which proved inconclusive as to the cause of death. Some days later a second and more detailed examination was performed on his body. This revealed that he had been beaten to death, battered about the head and body, resulting in broken bones and internal injuries, all of which contributed to his death.

Now that the police were absolutely convinced that Les's death was murder, they announced it to the media and began the hunt for those responsible. Detective Superintendent Chris Boarland was put in charge of the investigation and said, 'This has all the hallmarks of somebody who knew that he (Les) would be returning and was probably waiting for him to come home and then attack him. People knew he often used to carry significant amounts of cash with him.'

His wallet, the cheque and his cash were all missing, so robbery appeared the obvious motive. Police began to question customers who frequented the Maltsters Arms and other local pubs where Les was also known to drink. The usual forensic examination of his home was conducted, together with searches of the lanes and hedgerows along the route he took home. The police were particularly keen to trace the missing wallet.

Three weeks later and with no significant progress made, a press conference was held. Les's two children were present, Kathy having flown from Australia. She told the assembled reporters, 'Dad was very opinionated. I would describe him as a bit of a loveable rogue. Everyone who knew Les would say that he was an original, a one-off.' She continued, 'He could be a bit cantankerous. He had an opinion on most things. I am sure that he would have had something frank to say about Tony Blair.'

Martin, who worked in farming locally like his father, also spoke. 'A few people disliked him, but most people got on with him,' he said. 'It is hard to think that someone would have disliked him enough to want to kill him.' Kathy was keen to stress that she believed this was a robbery that had gone wrong, as opposed to a pre-meditated murder. She and Martin offered a reward of £10,000 for information leading to the arrest and conviction of those responsible.

A week later the police made a fresh appeal in relation to Les's missing wallet. A motorist had reported seeing a tan wallet lying in the A39, the main road that passes the front of Les's house. This sighting was apparently near to Tregilders Farm and soon after the killing. A police spokesman said, 'We don't know for certain that it was Les's wallet but we are obviously very keen to trace it. It may be that someone has picked it up and not realised its significance to our inquiries; we would very much like to hear from anyone who knows anything about it.' Extensive searches of the area were carried out but to no avail.

The police were not getting the level of assistance from the public that they had hoped for. Responses to appeals for information were described as 'disappointing'. The local media, however, showed considerable interest. As there had not been a murder in this tiny village for centuries many column inches were filled with the details. One newspaper quoted an unnamed friend of Les; he told the paper that Les had foreseen his own death. 'I had known Les for 30 years and he knew that it was coming. He telephoned a few weeks ago to say he wanted to meet up with all his friends before he died. I asked him why he was saying this. He said because of the burglary at his house he was having to barricade himself in his bedroom. He kept guns with him there because they were coming back for him.' He concluded, 'He knew some people were out to get him. Sadly they have.' Martin dismissed these claims as 'rubbish'.

On Tuesday, 10 September 2002, Les's funeral was held. The service was meant to be private. Nonetheless, mourners packed the St Kew parish church for a service officiated by Father Michael Bartlett. Some of the investigating officers were present, and afterwards Father Bartlett told the press, 'We must put our trust in God and pray that the police can bring the evil perpetrator who murdered Les to justice. I know that the family will not be able to rest until this happens.'

By now the police had scaled down the investigating team from over 40 to 25 officers. Some 900 statements had been taken, mostly from local people, but inquiries were said to be continuing 'at full pelt'.

By November, results of the forensic examinations carried out at the scene were being dispatched from the laboratory to the police. Traces of DNA had been found on some of Les's outer clothing. DNA is short for Deoxyribonucleic Acid; it is a complex chemical found in virtually every cell in the human body and it carries within it genetic information unique to an individual. DNA can be extracted from any cells that contain a nucleus. These include cells found in blood, semen, saliva and hair.

Once a sample of DNA is found, scientists at the laboratories of the Forensic Science Service have a variety of chemical processes that they can use to draw up a profile. Then by matching these profiles a person can be linked to or eliminated from an inquiry.

An item of clothing that Les was wearing at the time of his murder had recently been purchased from a shop in the nearby town of Wadebridge. Staff at the shop had DNA samples taken from them in order that their DNA could be compared to that found at the scene. Any such comparison would ordinarily enable the police to eliminate that person as a suspect, as there would be a legitimate reason for their DNA being found on the clothing.

A sample is taken from a person using a small plastic stick with a compressed cotton wool swab. This is rubbed against the inside of a person's mouth in order to obtain cells that will contain their DNA. It is a painless process. The swab is sealed in a small plastic tube and labelled. The tube and a barcode sticker unique to each sample are then placed in a tamper-proof clear plastic bag, along with the details of the person from whom the sample has been taken and of the officer who took it. It is then sent to the laboratory for analysis. It is vital that these procedures are meticulously carried out in order to ensure the integrity of each sample.

Twelve months of detective work had failed to bring anyone to justice for Les's murder, so an anniversary appeal was launched by the police a year on from the crime. By now the statement count was 1,000. The number of inquiries carried out totalled 2,000. The second in command of the investigation Detective Inspector Dee Peake said, 'The information we have so far suggests that it is a local person who is responsible.' Her boss, Detective Superintendent Boarland, was forced to admit that the delay between finding Les's body and the launch of the murder investigation could be crucial. He said, 'Losing two weeks has got to make it tougher for people to remember.' When questioned by journalists whether vital evidence might have been lost, he said, 'Only time will tell how much difference those days made.'

In August 2003, Kathy got on the phone from Australia to BBC Radio Cornwall. She told them, 'Time is going on and I suppose I am quite frustrated by the fact that no one has been prosecuted. I'm hopeful that the police will continue the investigation and they'll bring it to some sort of conclusion. It's just like an unresolved and outstanding issue. I'm just hoping to come to Cornwall some time in the near future and see whoever it was brought to justice.'

November 2003 saw this area shocked once again with the murders of Graham and Carol Fisher, and Joan Roddam. Devon and Cornwall police were under huge pressure. Their resources were stretched, and the media and residents were seeking reassurance. Four retired senior officers – two Detective Superintendents and two Detective Chief Inspectors – all ex-Devon and Cornwall men, were drafted in to help with these murders, or, in police speak, were 'recruited on a temporary basis to assist in the review of the current major investigations being carried out by the force'. The reaction to this news was varied. Some saw it as an admission that the police could not cope. Others viewed it as a sensible use of experienced personnel who would bring old-style coppering techniques to these investigations.

In any event, the two-year anniversary came around in April 2004 with still no significant progress. Somewhat predictably, the police said, 'We remain committed to solving his murder. There are a number of ongoing active lines of inquiry, and we are confident of finding the person responsible.'

I was beginning to find my way around this part of north Cornwall quite well. I was researching the Joan Roddam case as well as Les's murder during the same trip, so I spent much time driving from village to village meeting various sources of information, and occasionally visiting the nearby market town of Wadebridge.

I had an appointment to meet a local journalist at my bed and breakfast accommodation, and with an hour to wait I decided to read the local papers. I never cease to marvel at how issues vary from community to community in this wonderfully diverse island nation of ours, but what I read here about one particular local tradition took me by surprise. Among articles about boat building, elections for the Harbour Commission and the naming and shaming of locals who had fallen foul of the law, were numerous letters expressing outrage in the strongest terms the editor could print. The letter writers were all directing their anger towards the Devon and Cornwall Constabulary. In the town of Padstow on every Boxing Day and New Year, many local people take to the streets in colourful costumes, play musical instruments, sing songs and collect money for charity. This tradition has existed for decades and there may be nothing particularly unusual about that. However, what makes this celebration unusual in 21st-century Britain is that the participants blacken their faces and call it 'Darkie Day'.

The Chief Constable had seen fit to deploy many officers to the procession when it was last held, and had also decided to have the participants, including many children, videoed. An unconfirmed rumour went around that said the police had received a complaint about the event and that they were filming it in order to forward the footage to the Crown Prosecution Service, so that they could decide if any race laws had been contravened. Local people were outraged by this. I was told that 'Darkie Day' was held to commemorate a rescue centuries ago by local people of the African crew of a ship that had become shipwrecked off the Cornish coast. The black survivors had been saved and taken into the homes of Cornish people. 'How could it possibly be racist then?' complained a man to me later. People further expressed dismay at the expensive deployment of so many police officers on bank holidays when the cops would be paid at double time.

People feared that a part of their local history was under threat and, like communities all over the country, were critical of their local force. 'Try getting a copper to video the yobs smashing things up on a Friday night,' said one man to me, 'or getting them to solve a murder, eh. No chance. Then when people go out and enjoy themselves by way of a trouble-free tradition that has happened for years, they turn out in their droves.'

Another local tradition that was soon to be outlawed and which also received plenty of local media coverage was the hunting of foxes with hounds. Not surprisingly, many people were keen to give me their views on that as well, and they were not happy about it.

I decided to pay a visit to the Maltsters Arms. It had earned itself an entry in the 2005 edition of *The Good Pub Guide* but was virtually empty except for a couple eating and one man at the bar. I started to picture the Les I had heard about drinking here. He had, however, only used the Maltsters Arms as his local for a few months prior to his death.

A few more customers trickled in and I spoke to them. Like everywhere else I was to go locally, most of them knew Les. I quickly managed to empty the bar when I informed people what I was doing, and one customer menacingly said to me as he left, 'Make sure you lock your door tonight.' This was after I had perhaps unwisely told him where I was staying. He wasn't scary enough to put me off though, and in the absence of anyone to talk to I made my way to the pub that had previously been Les's local.

The St Kew Inn is a truly magnificent pub. It is grand-looking from the outside and very traditional inside. It appears to have been unchanged for centuries. Antique and comfortable furniture sits on a Delabole slate floor. A wide range of cask beers is available along with modern lagers and fine wines. It is situated in the centre of yet another tiny village, St Kew, and like the Maltsters Arms is only two miles from Les's home. For many years he had drunk there, usually perched on a stool at the bar. But somewhat sadly he had been barred from drinking there by the landlord following incidents when he had been rude to staff and customers. In fact, his behaviour had become so bad that when people drove into the pub car park and saw Les's Land Rover they would immediately drive off and find somewhere else to drink. In this part of the country almost every village has a decent pub with way above average food, wine and beers. Hence competition for custom is stiff, and the landlord of the St Kew Inn could not afford to have a grumpy, rude and obnoxious man driving away potential customers.

Many people remember Les as a happier drinker in years gone by. He would often have to repeat the jokes he told so that people understood them, but it was rumoured that a Cornish comedian named 'Jethro' was a friend and gleaned some comic ideas from him. Les also loved having a bet with people over dares. He would strike a wager with any person foolish enough to take him up on various challenges. Sometimes it was arm wrestling; he was only five-foot four, but he was stocky and powerful because of all the physical work involved in his farming. On other occasions a wager could relate to the consumption of large amounts or unusual types of alcohol or food. One friend of many years was laughing hysterically as he told me of the time he saw Les swallow a whole live fish, head first, and this was not a goldfish but something much larger plucked straight from the sea. Some of the details of this story were a little patchy, but his friend's tears of laughter convinced me his recollection was genuine.

Les was also a keen follower of local rugby club the Wadebridge Camels and was known to lead the clubhouse antics on many an occasion.

One part of his life upon which all people agreed was his work. He had a solid reputation as a hard-working and respected farmer. Rumour had it that he obtained the finance for his first farm during the 1940s and 1950s by shooting rabbits. He averaged between 80,000 and 100,000 rabbits a year – that's as many as 300 a day, seven days a week! Most of these were sent by train to towns and cities, some as far afield as London. The fact he had made his money through hard work was something he was proud of.

He was an astute businessman as well and in later years was well aware of farming subsidies that he could become eligible for. These are given to farmers and landowners under a European Union agreement known as the Common Agricultural Policy. This policy enables some of the wealthiest people in the country to pick up vast sums of money. In the year 2003–2004, the Queen received £545,897 for her farming interests at Sandringham and Windsor, and in the same year the Prince of Wales got £134,938 for his Duchy of Cornwall estate. At some point in his life, Les had been a Duchy tenant and did not have a decent word to say about HRH The Prince of Wales.

How the policy works is that the more land you own and the more farm animals you keep, or the more cereal you grow, the more money you get. Needless to say this policy is not popular with all. As I discovered, some non-farming residents of north Cornwall are distinctly unhappy with the system. Les often boasted of receiving such payments, and some believe that the cheque he had with him that night in the Maltsters Arms was a farming subsidy cheque. Les was also known to rent out some of his land for others to cultivate, especially as he got older, and another rumour was that the cheque was for rent.

Les was also famed for his hatred of paying money to any person he regarded as an establishment figure. He hated paying tax, and resented parting with even one penny to the taxman. Not long before he died, he apparently stormed out of his solicitor's office, having delivered a tirade about how slow, useless and expensive he considered them to be.

Some people I met had known Les since his childhood. Apparently his father had been a strict disciplinarian and prone to taking his belt to Les on the occasions that he misbehaved. This may have had some bearing on his later life as people regaled me with tales of Les's own violent behaviour. I don't particularly like speaking ill of the dead and many of the stories I heard I have chosen not to include, as I cannot corroborate them, and in any event they are largely irrelevant. But the following story illustrates how he had the ability to make himself unpopular. Les came into a pub one night and told everyone who would listen that he had a terrier dog that he was struggling to control. In order to punish it he said he had inserted a firework into its rear and lit it. The subsequent explosion apparently killed the animal. People were sickened to hear him tell this tale. Of course it could have been made up by Les or have been a drunken yarn. In any event, it did not win him any friends.

While a source who I will call 'Jim' was telling me this very tale, a young man in his 30s, about five-foot nine tall and of average build, came into the pub where we were having a pint and walked past us up to the bar. He was an unremarkable man to look at, but by the look on Jim's face it was obvious that all was not well. Jim immediately changed the subject away from Les and so we conversed about a new topic, which was the price of local fish. Jim and I both went to the toilet soon afterwards, and as I kept my eye on the door I asked him what was going on. 'That guy who has just walked in is a bully. I don't want him to know you and I are talking about Les,' he said. 'Look, it's not good for you and me to be seen talking together. We'll speak later.' I returned to the bar and saw that a local magistrate and his wife, who had been pointed out to me earlier, were now talking to the man who so obviously struck fear into Jim.

Fortunately the tough guy did not stay long, and Jim and I were able to resume our conversation. I had to ask him once again if he thought the bully boy was responsible for Les's death, but he would only say that people believed whoever was responsible must be local, and that nobody wanted the same to happen to them. I pointed out how unlikely that was, as surely the unpopularity of Les had been a major factor in the attack upon him. He agreed but said people were very wary as the killer was still at large. Fear of crime appears to be as much of a factor in the lives of some country dwellers as it is for those who live in some of the worst crime-ridden sink estates of our inner cities.

I have to say that some other people did not seem in the slightest bit concerned over Les's murder. People would express to me their shock and revulsion over the shooting and battering of the Fisher couple in nearby Wadebridge, crimes for which two people had been arrested, but merely shrugged their shoulders when discussing Les's murder. It was as though they had graded murder into those more and less serious. I was beginning to think that maybe my attitude, which is that murder is murder, was wrong. Of course I understand the outrage and great sense of loss and fear that a child killing creates, I just believe that no matter the age of the victim or method of killing it is always a crime that should be worthy of the same resources being applied to it, and that if any such crime remains unsolved, it should be of concern to us all. After all, no matter who or how a murderer has killed, do we want them in our midst?

Les had experienced his fair share of tragedy in life. About fifty years before his own murder, his brother had been shot and killed in what was referred to by some locally as an accident. No one was able to give me precise details, and given the passage of time perhaps that is not surprising. What was surprising was that more than one person told me that it had been anything but an accident. Legend has it that Les had shot his brother in a rage.

If the shooting was a tragic accident, and let's be clear Les was never charged with any offence in relation to it, then tragedy was to strike him again. Two decades later his son Kevin was killed in a drink-driving accident. 'There but for the grace of God go I,' said a former friend of Kevin who told me of the fatal crash. 'Everybody does it. It's a way of life round here. If

152

you want to have a social life, you have to go out. If you're going to go out, you have to drive. If you want to have a drink, you have to drink and drive, so it's a recreational hazard.'

I visited Les's home twice, in daylight and at night, but as it is now a family home I was not able to view the inside. It is a detached stone building with a gated driveway and an enormous barn to the left as you look at it. Les was not renowned for closing his gate, and there is ample parking space for cars, including places where a car could easily be concealed. Inside the barn is a mass of farming machinery and equipment. A four-foot-high stone wall borders the front of the house and garden. Hedgerows and fencing mark the borders around the sides and back. To the right of the property are open fields, and some derelict outbuildings are to the rear. Any person wishing to lie in wait for Les's return would have had no problem finding suitable cover. Tregilders Farm is not overlooked by any other properties.

There is no pavement at the front of the farmhouse. Any pedestrians have to walk on a grass verge. On 5 November 2003, Les's son Martin was in Tregilders Farm clearing out some of his late father's possessions. This was the day that the Fisher couple were murdered nearby. He saw a person walk past the house, and later heard a police appeal for information that related to a person of a similar description. He reported the sighting to the police and became a potential witness in yet another murder case.

The farmhouse had been an easy target providing rich pickings for burglars the previous October. While Les had been out drinking as normal one night, thieves entered his home and stole his safe, which contained £47,000 in cash. They also stole a number of paintings and other valuables. Les was extremely upset by this and had apparently taken to sleeping with a shotgun by his bed. He was a legal and licensed shotgun holder, but may not have remained so had the police become aware of the many conversations he had with friends, when he often stated that if burglars entered his property when he was there, he would have no qualms about shooting them.

Another farmer who lived alone and who had also suffered previous attacks upon his property was the Norfolk farmer Tony Martin. Just like Les, local people had mixed opinions of him. When Tony Martin's farmhouse was attacked by two burglars in August 1999, he shot them. Fred Barras, who was 16 at the time, died. The other burglar, Brendon Fearon, received shotgun injuries for which he later tried to sue Mr Martin. Tony Martin was jailed for life for the murder of Barras in April 2000. This sparked a national outcry and at a later appeal Tony Martin's conviction for murder was quashed and reduced to one of manslaughter, for which he received five years' imprisonment. Fearon received three years for the burglary of Mr Martin's home.

The debate still rages regarding how much force homeowners are permitted to use against intruders. In Les's case I believe he and not his home was the intended target, but his case, along with the Roddam murder and other reported attacks, highlight the issue of attacks upon vulnerable people living in remote or isolated dwellings. Sadly, my advice to anyone living in such circumstances would be to install as many security measures as your budget will permit. Fit the best door and window locks available. If possible, install CCTV and an alarm system linked to an exchange that will notify the police in the event of the alarm being activated. Ensure that the alarm has a proper system of zones, so that as you retire to bed the entire property except for the room in which you sleep is alarmed. Supplement this with a readily accessible panic button near to where you sleep. To those of you who believe you cannot afford such a system I would advise you look at any possessions of value that you own. Seriously consider selling them to raise the funds. Sadly, it is now clear that with these types of attack becoming ever more common, the owners of such properties must take whatever precautions necessary to deter these unscrupulous criminals.

I drove up and down the A39, which runs in front of Tregilders Farm, many times. I remain sceptical as to whether anybody would have been able to see clearly something as small as a wallet lying in this main road while travelling at speed. It was this alleged sighting near to Tregilders Farm that led the police to make a number of public appeals relating to it and also led them to carry out a thorough search of the area, all of which were to no avail. I have wondered as to whether this reported sighting is entirely genuine. Unfortunately, murder enquiries and other major investigations are sometimes hampered by individuals who report false sightings of persons, cars, or anything else that they may have seen in the media or in appeal posters. I would also have been surprised if the perpetrator had dumped Les's wallet near to the scene of the crime.

Equally as annoying for detectives are the cranks who familiarise themselves with every piece of information that they can from the media, and then present themselves at police stations wanting to confess to murders they did not commit. The first ever conviction in the UK using DNA evidence cleared a suspect who had admitted to carrying out a murder that it was later proved he could not have been responsible for. Two schoolgirls were murdered in the Leicestershire village of Narborough. In 1983, 15-year-old Lynda Mann was found raped and murdered. Semen was found on her body, which upon analysis was found to belong to a man with type-A blood that had a particular enzyme profile possessed by only 10 per cent of the adult male population. Despite this precise information, the police had been unable to find whoever was responsible.

Three years later, another 15-year-old girl, Dawn Ashworth, was found strangled and sexually assaulted. Semen was also recovered from her body, which when matched with that found on Lynda was shown to come from the same person. A local lad was the main suspect, and when arrested he admitted killing Dawn but denied any involvement in Lynda's murder. Analysis of his DNA, however, showed that he was not responsible for either killing. That lad should be very grateful for the advances in forensic science that continue today. Not so many years ago he would have been charged on the basis of his confession, and, as he revealed information during that confession that was not widely known, he most likely would have been convicted. Unfortunately, recent criminal history has been littered with similar miscarriages of justice.

The Leicestershire Police in their efforts to find the girls' killers conducted the world's first DNA mass screening. Some 5,000 local men were asked to provide samples for analysis. One man was overheard boasting of how he had masqueraded as somebody else when giving his sample. A female work colleague of this indiscreet man overheard his conversation and reported it to police. They then arrested both the impostor and the man who he had pretended to be, Colin Pitchfork. Pitchfork's DNA sample showed that it was his semen found on the girls. In 1998, he was sentenced to life imprisonment for the two murders.

Mass DNA screening is a useful tool used in many murder investigations, and in Les's case the police were obviously in possession of some DNA evidence, hence the reason that samples were taken from the clothing shop. I am therefore puzzled as to why mass screening of all members of the local population has not been done in this case. The village in which Les lived has a small population, as do the surrounding villages. Police have stated they believe the killer to be local, so mass screening would seem to be entirely appropriate. At worst it is a cost effective way of eliminating large numbers of people from an inquiry. This occurs when their DNA is compared to that found at the scene, and is found not to match. At best it may identify the suspect.

Even in cases where the amount of DNA recovered is very small, more sophisticated tests have been developed that enable scientists to draw up a profile of an offender. This test is known as a Low Copy Number test and has successfully identified offenders from a few cells left on items as small as a toothpick.

People were anxious that I noted concerns they had about some aspects of the investigation into Les's murder. Many people expressed bewilderment at the two-week gap between the finding of Les's body and the announcement that there was to be a murder inquiry, and also that two post-mortems were needed.

In any case, here are my thoughts. Les was an undeniably

high-profile character in his local area, liked or loathed, and known more often than not to have a lot of cash on him. Those who knew him, and that was virtually everyone, knew where he lived. They also knew he liked to drink a few pints and would invariably be home soon after closing. People were aware that he was not a fit youngster and, while he was a strong man in his younger days, at 71 years of age he would not present too much of a challenge to a younger person intent on robbing him. He therefore was a relatively easy target, and as a result I believe someone decided to relieve him of his wallet. In doing so they used enough force to kill him and deny him his dotage.

Les being Les, I hope he had the chance to tell his assailant what he thought of him. I am surprised that no one has yet been charged with this crime, and as I prepared to leave Cornwall the weather changed. The beautiful spring days I had enjoyed with blue skies and sunshine were replaced by cloud, rain and a sharp drop in temperature. I had one last conversation with someone who had helped me considerably, and when we discussed the weather change she said, 'You see, the weather gods don't want you to go; they want you to stay until you have solved these cases.' I may well be back.

CHAPTER SEVEN

MILLY

Heathside School describes itself as a Foundation Community Technology College, teaching children of both sexes from the ages of 11 to 18. It occupies a position half way down Brooklands Lane, a narrow road with picturesque cottages and substantial detached houses. Beyond the school the road leads to playing fields and a farm, and thereafter is a dead end.

Opposite the school is Weybridge Cemetery, a beautifully maintained site with a delightful chapel. At lunchtimes, pupils from across the road can be found polluting their lungs with a sneaky cigarette, away from the prying eyes of teaching staff. When school finishes for the day, children mingle there or use it as a cut through, chattering to their pals about whatever takes their fancy, taking no notice of the many hundreds of deceased who are buried around them.

Tragically, many of these youngsters have had to face the

harsh reality of death, for on Thursday, 21 March 2002, a fellow pupil, 13-year-old Amanda Dowler, known to all as 'Milly', disappeared, only to be found murdered some months later.

There surely is no crime so vile, or one that engenders such feelings of revulsion among right-minded people, as that of the abduction, possible sexual assault, and murder of a child. As with all the cases in this book I endeavoured to make contact with the police investigating the crime, the Surrey Constabulary. They are the lead agency in this investigation, and despite many phone calls and emails I have had no response from them. So, as was usually the way with cases in this book, my research was wholly reliant upon my own experiences, visits to places of relevance, observations and inquiries carried out at these sites, and information received from journalistic and other sources.

I started my research by retracing Milly's last known movements. She was seen on CCTV leaving school that day at 3.07pm. She was wearing her school uniform, which consisted of a dark blue blazer, grey skirt, white shirt with school tie, and a blue jumper. She was carrying a beige rucksack. She then walked with friends to Weybridge railway station.

This walk would have taken her either through or around woodland that leads to the station. The slightly shorter route is through the woods, and this route would most likely have taken her past the gate of Brooklands College, a further education establishment, and the Hand and Spear pub. Then she would have had to walk a few yards through a pay-and-display car park. It took me 12 minutes to walk this route, which is mostly uphill. For Milly this walk took 16 minutes, as she was next seen on CCTV at the station at 3.23pm. By now she was not wearing her jumper. The day she disappeared was a sunny day, so I don't believe there is anything unusual about that, as she probably got warm during the walk to Weybridge station.

She boarded a train that was ultimately bound for Waterloo. This train would have started its journey from either Basingstoke in Hampshire or Woking in Surrey. A Basingstoke train would have stopped at seven other stations before Weybridge, including Fleet in Hampshire. The Woking train would have stopped at only two stations beforehand. Other trains that use this line but do not stop at Weybridge originate from Alton in Hampshire and stop at the garrison town of Aldershot on their journey to Waterloo. These frequent trains with their speedy journeys into central London, coupled with decent road links, make the green and leafy town of Weybridge, Surrey, one of the most affluent and desirable parts of the country.

Milly's journey was to be for one stop only, to Walton on Thames. This is another affluent area. A three-bedroom semi-detached house here can set you back more than £400,000. The area has a number of smart restaurants and delicatessens that serve a wide range of cuisines from around the world, and the large number of other small businesses that I saw seemed to be thriving.

Under normal circumstances Milly would have stayed on the train for two stops until she reached Hersham, a station less than half a mile from her home. But on this day she had decided to go with a friend to the Travellers Café, a rather uninspiring eatery that occupies a position on platform one of Walton on Thames station. This is the platform at which Milly would have disembarked. She and her friend shared a plate of chips before leaving. Unfortunately, the CCTV cameras on this station were not working at the time — apparently the system was being repaired and no provision had been made for a temporary replacement.

From here she should have made the one-mile walk to the family home in the desirable road named Walton Park. What happened after she left the station has been subject to much speculation, but what is known is that she did not make it home. It was not in character for Milly to disappear. She had no history of running away, of delinquent behaviour or teenage rebellion. When she was reported missing to police, the full wheels of a vulnerable missing person inquiry swung into motion. Over a hundred officers began searching for her, supported by police dogs and a helicopter. Members of the public volunteered to help and were deployed to search wasteland near to her home, working alongside police officers. Police marine units searched nearby rivers.

Forensic teams began a search of the family home looking for clues, and Milly's computer was taken for examination. This was in order to see if she had made contact in internet chat rooms with anybody who could be connected to her disappearance. Thousands of posters were rapidly printed and were distributed by anyone willing to help, including her school friends. They were attached to cars, lampposts and trees, and distributed in shops, pubs, clubs and restaurants – anywhere that it was hoped might generate a response.

The media attended a press conference held on Sunday, 24 March in their droves. Milly's dad Bob, a 50-year-old IT consultant, and her mum Sally, a 42-year-old mathematics teacher who taught at Milly's school, made emotional pleas for the safe return of their daughter. Bob was asked if he believed Milly was still alive. He said, 'We just desperately hope she is. It is the only thing that keeps us going.' He went on to describe his beloved Milly. 'She is very special; we couldn't wish for a lovelier daughter,' he said. 'She's got a great sense of fun, plays the saxophone and is very musical. We bought her a karaoke machine for Christmas. She's always dancing and singing in the sitting room.' The singer Will Young, who had recently sprung to prominence courtesy of the television talent show *Pop Idol* and who Milly had gone to see in concert the week before she disappeared, also made an appeal. He asked her to go home or to contact her family.

A close friend, Cara Dawson, had been with Milly at Walton on Thames railway station, but she had decided not to join her for the plate of chips. She also spoke to the press. The girls' families were good friends, and Milly had holidayed with Cara and her parents. Appealing to anyone who might be holding Milly against her will, she said, 'She has not done anything to you. She doesn't deserve it.' Every newspaper and TV channel covered the story on a daily basis.

Two days later, on Tuesday, 26 March, a reconstruction of Milly's last known movements was filmed for broadcasting on *Crimewatch*. It was rapidly edited in order that it could be transmitted two days later on the one-week anniversary of her disappearance. Surrey Police revealed that the Royal Air Force was to join the hunt, flying reconnaissance missions, and that the number of officers engaged in the searches would be boosted to 150.

The *Crimewatch* programme went out and attracted over 250 calls from members of the public. One caller rang in to say they had found a purse similar to the one Milly had been carrying. This was retrieved by the police and shown to her parents but was not their daughter's.

A few days passed with little more information being released by the police, but then on Thursday, 4 April, two weeks after Milly's disappearance, they held another press conference. Detective Superintendent Alan Sharp, the officer in charge of the investigation, released details of three separate sightings of a girl, believed to be Milly, which had come from different witnesses. The first witness, a friend, said they saw Milly at the junction of Station Avenue and Rydens Road at 4.03pm. She would have completed about a third of her walk home at this point.

The next witness, a male motorist, said he saw a girl matching Milly's description, walking along crying in Rydens Road near to the junction with Sidney Road. This is only 150 metres from the previous sighting and on the route she would have taken home. The third witness, another male motorist, said he had also seen a girl matching Milly's description standing in Rydens Road at the junction with Walton Park, the road in which she lived. He had noticed that this girl was crying.

Detective Superintendent Sharp said a blue Saab car had been seen in the vicinity and that the driver had apparently been in conversation with a young woman. He asked for this person to come forward. The police were clearly considering that Milly might have disappeared with somebody that she knew, as Sharp went on to say, 'There is nothing in her history to suggest she planned to go off on her own. If she has been abducted, a girl of 13 is far more likely to go with someone she knew than someone she didn't. If there was a struggle on a day as sunny as this day was, it is surprising that no one saw anything.'

On this last point I must agree. I have spent a lot of time in and around this area, especially at the time of day when Milly disappeared. As you exit Walton on Thames railway station there is a large Jaguar car dealership on the opposite side of the road to your left. Alongside that is a large pub called the Ashley Park. From certain vantage points in the pub it is possible to see the comings and goings of the station. In a parade of businesses alongside the station there is a minicab office, a florists, a dry cleaners and a barbershop. Opposite the station, on both sides of the road, there are bus stops where services start and terminate. These buses convey passengers to various locations, including the local shopping centre and Heathrow Airport.

On the same side of Station Avenue as the railway station there used to be a tyre and exhaust fitting business that has since been demolished. There is a sizeable pay-and-display car park, a telephone box and a large office building, Walton Court, part of the Unilever foods empire. On the opposite side of the road there are blocks of desirable-looking flats, the highest of which is four stories, and a few houses, all reached via four interlinking roads that form a loop and all exit upon Station Avenue. One of these roads is Copenhagen Way. It is 150 metres from the railway station and leads to Collingwood Place. As well as the flats and houses there are some rows of garages that are all neat and well maintained. These roads have some parking spaces but they are set aside for residents. Yellow lines restrict parking on all other parts of these roads. This does not mean to say that people always abide by these restrictions.

On one visit I saw a couple sitting in a car parked illegally; they were talking and smoking, and as soon as they saw me coming they started the engine and drove off. A suspect may have waited here to pounce, but, although this residential area is usually quiet during the day, they would have been taking a huge risk in that they would have stood out and could easily have been noticed by any attentive passer-by. The remainder of the area around the station is a hive of activity on any weekday, especially around the time of day that Milly was walking home.

Two days later the CCTV images that showed Milly leaving her school and at Weybridge railway station were released in a bid to jog people's memories. On Sunday, 7 April, the police revealed they had been searching woodland near Weybridge. They also said that the release of the CCTV images had produced a significant number of calls from the public. They had now received well over a thousand calls in total but had no clear leads.

On Sunday, 21 April, details of a 'friendship book' that Milly co-wrote with school pal Hannah McDonald were released. The pair had become friends on a school trip to Germany in 1999, and thereafter they wrote notes and placed photographs in this 'Winnie the Pooh' book. Hannah said to the press, 'Milly is a loyal friend. She is one-of-a-kind and I hope that being reminded of our happy memories will help bring her back.' Ominously, the police admitted that they had so far failed to unearth a single clue as to where she might be.

Five weeks after her disappearance, the body of a female was found floating in the River Thames at Sunbury by two cyclists. The scene of the discovery was only two miles from Milly's home, so DNA and dental checks were carried out on the corpse in order to establish if it was her. The body had been in the river for some time and was badly decomposed. Milly's parents were informed of the find and had to endure tortuous hours waiting for the results. It turned out to be the body of an elderly lady who had been missing from home for over a year.

Detective Superintendent Sharp had some uncomfortable

questions from the press to deal with after he had released the details of the body in the Thames. He was grilled as to whether the investigation should be reclassified as a murder inquiry, rather than a search for a missing person. He defended the position of the Surrey Constabulary by saying they had been committed to finding Milly from the outset, and that the investigation had been 'painstakingly thorough'.

Young Hannah McDonald bravely made an appearance on ITV's breakfast programme *GMTV* on Thursday, 25 April. Watching her made for emotional viewing as she pleaded, 'Milly, if you're out there, please, please call your parents or me or anyone you know, just so we know you're fine. And if anyone is holding Milly, please let her go. We love her so much and any day without her is hell – hell let loose. We really want her back. Please give her back.'

At the end of April a woman was arrested on suspicion of harassing the Dowler family. They had been receiving hoax telephone calls at their home and had reported them to the police. A 20-year-old from Tewkesbury in Gloucestershire was arrested and released on bail. Unfortunately, this was not to be the last time that they were harassed.

The media were still covering the case with fervent interest, and in early May the *Sun* offered a £100,000 reward for information that led to finding Milly. This must have sent shockwaves through the Surrey Constabulary, as it prompted the Chief Constable Denis O'Connor to state, 'We are grateful for the practical support at this critical point in time. We think that there is someone out there who knows something that they are not telling us. We sincerely hope that this fresh approach will spark someone into telling us any secrets about Milly that they know.' Quite which 'critical point in time' and which 'secrets about Milly' he was referring to I have not been able to discover. Milly had now been missing for six weeks.

The police still thought some of her school friends had secrets to offer up. An inspector was sent into Heathside School and told all the children in her year, 'We want to uncover everything you know about why Amanda may have disappeared. We want to know about your private thoughts and conversations with Amanda.' By now the tally of phone calls from the public to the police was over 3,000. They had taken 750 statements, interviewed over 100 of her friends, and completed over 100 searches of various sites. Yet still they believed a 13- or 14-year-old friend might hold the clue as to why she was missing.

The police seemed to like Sundays for their press conferences. This may have been a sensible tactic designed to maximise publicity on what is usually the slowest news day of the week. On 5 May they held another one. A statement from the Dowlers was read out and a new photograph of Milly was released. The police declared that over a hundred telephone calls had been received since the *Sun* had offered its reward, and they told the press that they thought Milly might have been secretly communicating with somebody via an internet chat room. They had also checked out a possible sighting of Milly buying euros in a post office in Ipswich the previous day, but this turned out to be another child.

The first arrest in connection with Milly's disappearance came in the middle of May when a 36-year-old labourer was arrested in Chertsey, some three miles from Milly's home. He was living in a house undergoing renovation and was believed to be part of a team of builders carrying out that work. A white Rover car was taken away for forensic examination. The house was searched, as was a garage at the end of the garden. He was soon released without charge. Another arrest came on 13 June when a 52-year-old Surrey man was detained, questioned, and released.

Tuesday, 25 June 2002 would have been Milly's 14th birthday. By this time the police had accepted that there was little chance of her being found alive, and they had told her parents 'to expect the worst'. Bob and Sally released a written statement saying, 'Her birthday is going to be so hard for the whole family, for our friends and for her friends. No one really knows what to do. For example, should they send cards? Any family occasions are really hard, even other people's birthdays. We go to send them a card, and then it hits us, who do we sign it from? Now we just put "The Dowlers". The whole concept of wishing someone a happy birthday is very hard to reconcile.' Bob spoke of the anguish that any sort of occasion brought. 'Last weekend was really hard, being Father's Day,' he said. 'Gemma came downstairs and gave me a card. It took me completely unawares. There are normally two cards. It was a bad day.'

Friday, 12 July signalled a major change in the information that the police had been releasing. They stated that they now thought Milly had been taken in a 'chance abduction', and that it might have been carried out by someone using trickery in order to get the schoolgirl into a vehicle. This arose as they revealed that a witness had definitely seen Milly walking along Station Avenue from the railway station, but that Milly had not been seen on film retrieved from a CCTV system attached to an office building further along that same road. This therefore created a 60-second 'window' during which they believed she had been snatched. This would also mean that the teenage girl described by earlier witnesses as crying and seen nearer to her home had not been Milly.

The police were keen to trace people that had been sighted on the CCTV footage, and these included a group of women, a cyclist, a blonde female and a man with a guitar. These people were traced and interviewed as possible witnesses. The police also described this CCTV footage as a 'key piece of evidence' and revealed that they had sent the tape to the FBI for enhancement, although this process had already been carried out in the UK and so they did not hold out too much hope of a result.

Detective Chief Superintendent Craig Denholm was now in charge of the investigation; he also had to defend claims that the investigation had been bungled. He described the case as 'unique and extremely challenging' and said, 'It is most unusual not to have any witness, body, scene or main suspect.' He said that the blue Saab had been eliminated from the inquiry but that he wished to trace a red car of which no more details were forthcoming.

I must admit to being amazed and angry that a girl could have been taken without anybody noticing in an area as busy as Station Avenue, especially at that time of day. However, when investigating a case such as this it should be borne in mind that the offender is likely to have planned his crime. I say 'he', as the vast majority of these types of crimes are committed by men. He had probably been looking for the opportunity to carry out this sort of offence for a while, and when it arose he used arrogance and confidence to coerce or force Milly into a vehicle.

I believe the police concentrated on the theory that she must have disappeared with somebody she knew for too long. I am a little surprised that the police thought it necessary to send an officer to Milly's school six weeks after she had been reported missing in an effort to encourage pupils to give up secrets the police thought they were still harbouring. Surely they would have told all they knew long before, when the seriousness of the situation was clearly apparent, though no doubt the police were determined to be extremely thorough.

On Monday, 29 July, the police made another arrest. This time a 47-year-old man from Walton on Thames was detained. He was later released without charge. Two months after receiving the CCTV footage, the FBI returned it to the Surrey Constabulary. They had succeeded in removing some blurring caused by the bright sunshine on the day. The tapes now showed a schoolgirl about the same age as Milly talking to the driver of a dark saloon car. This was seven minutes after the last known sighting of Milly and close to where that sighting occurred. Detective Chief Superintendent Denholm said he was '50 per cent sure' that it was Milly. He added, 'If it is her, this is massively significant, but that's the key question: is it her?' He went on to say, 'This footage is a key piece of evidence and, if it is Amanda, it raises a lot more questions. Most significantly did she know the person in the car? We are requesting the driver of the car to contact us as he may have valuable information that will help the inquiry.' It was suggested that this saloon car might have been a Honda Prelude or a Vauxhall Vectra.

A number of other cars were seen to pass this car while it was stopped, and an appeal went out to the drivers of those vehicles to come forward. In particular a white Mercedes, possibly a 190 or 300 series, was seen to swerve around the stationary saloon, and the police were keen to trace the driver of that car.

Less than a week after the release of the enhanced CCTV tapes, on Wednesday, 18 September, a couple were out picking wild mushrooms in Yateley Heath Woods. This is a large area of mixed woodland, sandwiched between the A30 and the M3 motorway near Fleet in Hampshire. Near to a footpath but in dense woodland they found skeletal remains and reported this to police the following day. Hampshire Police sealed off a large area around the site of the find in an effort to preserve any potential evidence. Dental checks and DNA tests were carried out and these confirmed that the remains were all that was left of Milly.

At this stage experts in forensic entomology may have been involved. This is the science of insects, and by examining any bugs such as flies, their larvae or eggs, or their remnants, it is often possible to determine the length of time a corpse has been at the site where it was found. Some insects prefer to feast on the fluids that leak from a corpse into the ground, so soil samples would have been taken for later examination. Forensic botany techniques may also have been deemed appropriate. Pollen or other minute plant samples may have been found at the scene that were not native to these woods and may have indicated a particular plant with which an offender might have come into contact, or have kept at home.

Milly's parents were informed about the fate that had befallen their daughter on Friday, 20 September. It was Bob's 51st birthday. The family drew the curtains of their home and locked themselves away in order to deal with their grief.

A hundred officers carried out a detailed search of the

woodland. It was the eve of the six-month anniversary of Milly's disappearance. Detective Chief Superintendent Denholm travelled to the site and liaised with his Hampshire colleagues.

Meanwhile, back in Walton on Thames, flowers and messages of condolence were left at the family home. Friends gathered and sobbed together. The press published many of the glowing tributes that were paid to Milly. In Hampshire, police appeals for witnesses went out. None of Milly's clothes or other possessions had been found in the woods and tracing these became a high priority. Once again a description of what she had been wearing and carrying was given out. A hut was rapidly put together in order to house the many flowers and other tributes that the public were wanting to lay, and a book of condolences was made available.

On Thursday, 26 September, Bob and Sally were accompanied by Detective Chief Superintendent Denholm as they visited the tribute hut. After that they were shown the place where Milly's remains had been found. Witnesses who had seen things of interest in this area started to come forward. One stated that they had seen a man in his late 40s carrying a shovel near to the Ely pub on the A30. This sighting was on the morning of Sunday, 24 March, and the man was described as wearing a thigh-length green parka jacket.

Another witness gave information described by Detective Chief Superintendent Denholm as 'very significant'. This witness said that on the day Milly disappeared he was driving his car south along Minley Road, a road that borders Yateley Heath Wood, at about 4.45pm. He saw a medium-sized car, one about the size of a Ford Escort or Mondeo, which was dark coloured and parked at an angle to the road at the gateway of

Minley Farm. He estimated the car to be eight to ten years old. Further down the same road he said he saw a large white van. He described it as being bigger than a Ford Transit and said it was parked at a 90-degree angle to the road. He also noticed a man walking from the front of the van to the driver's door, which was open. He described this man as white, aged in his 20s, of medium build with a round face, clean-shaven and with light brown hair.

It was what this witness had to say about his return trip up Minley Road at around 5pm that really got the police interested. The witness said that he was now travelling north and on his left he saw two men with a schoolgirl in a field. One of the men was immediately behind the girl and the other was about six feet away from her. She was described as wearing a dark blazer and a grey skirt or dress. He added that further up the road he overtook a dark-coloured car, a medium-sized saloon with two young men inside that was travelling very slowly. His last observation, which might or might not have been relevant, was that he saw a silver or grey Volvo at the entrance to Pennyhill Caravan Park. The occupants of this car were an elderly lady driver and a female passenger with long dark hair.

Denholm said of this witness's information, 'We have gone through every detail with the witness, including retracing the route with him, and are as sure as we can be of the details. However, we do not know for certain if it was Milly.' He went on to ask for any of the people mentioned by this witness to come forward. The woods remained closed to the public as a huge search continued.

If the girl this witness saw was Milly, whoever took her to the woods almost certainly travelled there directly from Walton on Thames. I have driven the various routes that could have been taken, and there is not a great deal of difference either in distance or in the amount of time that they take. The shortest journey is 23 miles. This route, however, entails driving through the built-up area of Weybridge before joining the M25 motorway at junction 11. From there it is a short trip to junction 12 where the M25 meets with the M3, and then a 14-mile trip down the M3 to junction 4a, which is signposted Fleet. Two miles from here is Yateley Heath Woods. This journey took me 28 minutes. I drove within the speed limit as I believe an offender would if he had either an abducted girl or a corpse with him in his vehicle. I think it unlikely that he would have wanted to bring attention to himself by driving erratically or at breakneck speed. Another route took me through Walton on Thames to junction one of the M3, and from there to Yateley Heath Woods. This journey was 30 miles and took me 40 minutes.

Had I abducted Milly, I would have taken the next route, as it did not entail driving through any town centres where the risk of being seen by a witness or of being filmed on CCTV would have been higher. I would have driven along Station Avenue, past Walton on Thames railway station, and soon joined the relatively open country route of the B365, Seven Hills Road. From there it is pretty plain sailing to junction ten of the M25, and then to the M3. This route is 28 miles and took me 35 minutes.

The area immediately around Yateley Heath Woods is rural, mainly common or farm land. The town of Yateley lies to the north, and Fleet to the south. Apart from occasional farmhouses, the nearest residential buildings are the Gibraltar Barracks and

Minley Manor, homes to a section of the British Army, the Royal Engineers. These buildings are heavily fortified and permanently guarded by soldiers with rifles. The military's influence on the area is inescapable, with many army vehicles and staff coming and going, and other personnel maintaining their fitness by running through the woodland often carrying heavy packs or logs. The public are prohibited from considerable sections of the woods courtesy of legislation entitled the Aldershot and District Military Lands Bye-laws of 1976. Under these laws, sections of land are designated as Ministry of Defence training areas, and numerous signs warn of the dangers of touching suspicious objects, which could turn out to be unexploded devices. Other warning signs read 'Danger, armed patrols and guard dogs, keep out'. Some even say 'Out of bounds to troops' – quite who is allowed in those parts I don't know.

A notable landmark that borders the woods is Blackbushe Airport, a relatively small aerodrome that houses light aircraft. This site also houses British Car Auctions and a Sunday market. Lay-bys and car parks are not a common sight around the borders of these woods, and a considerable degree of local knowledge would be a must for anyone wishing to park a vehicle and then dispose of a body. At all the points of entry to the woods that I found, it was necessary to climb over a stile or alternatively negotiate a barrier. Once in the woodland and away from the warning signs and the discarded rusted junk left by our forces, its beauty is inescapable. Vast high banks of wild rhododendrons flourish, and enormous spruce and pine reach into the sky. A few trees have been felled to create obstacles for the horses that are exercised here, but this has been done in a sympathetic manner, with consideration for the environment a priority. I pocketed a couple of fallen pinecones knowing that my youngest boys would enjoy painting them.

A rotting piece of police barrier tape dangling from a tree is the only remnant of the grim find here back in September 2002. I walked for hours around this area, pacing out the distances from possible parking places to where her remains were found and timing walks from the field where the schoolgirl had been seen to the same place. With a lack of information from the police about whether they believe Milly was killed in the woods or elsewhere, it is difficult to formulate a definitive theory. The police of course are entitled to withhold such information, but until someone stands trial for this offence we will not be able to find out their reasons for withholding it. What I would say is that only a person of some strength and fitness would have been able to transport a corpse from the parking spaces that are on the edges of the woods to the place where the remains were found.

Meanwhile, work on the CCTV footage that had shown the girl speaking to the driver of a car near Walton on Thames railway station had not stopped with the FBI enhancement. A British company, Kalagate Imagery Bureau from Cambridgeshire, had superimposed images of vehicles over the footage in an effort to positively identify the make of vehicle. It was now thought that the car was 'more than likely' a Mazda MX6. This was released to the press together with the fact that only 5,000 of these cars had been sold in the UK. Detective Chief Superintendent Denholm again appealed for the driver to come forward. The media continued to do their bit by giving this information plenty of coverage.

By now it was mid-November. Yateley Heath Woods were

finally being opened up to the public, and the horse riders, walkers, joggers, wildlife enthusiasts, families and dog walkers who had previously used the woods were able to enjoy them once again. They and motorists using adjoining roads were subjected to roadblocks and stop-checks by a team of 16 officers from Hampshire Police. Such checks are performed in an effort to trace witnesses who may be unaware that they possess relevant information until they are questioned. Six thousand cars were stopped in two days; car parks and lay-bys were also checked. No one complained and all were keen to do whatever they could to help the investigation.

Soon after Milly had first been reported missing, the police had carried out a thorough forensic search of her house. Her clothing had been taken for detailed examination, and in January 2003 it was revealed by police that the DNA of an unknown man had been found on one such article of clothing. This sample had been found to match DNA found on a coffee cup at the scene of a burglary at St Paul's Church in Ryhope, Sunderland. This church had been burgled on 31 October 2002. Detectives from Surrey travelled north and took samples from 46 members of the congregation and other people linked to the church. This find was described by Surrey Police as 'a very odd coincidence' and worthy of further investigation. In June 2003 the police ruled out any link between Milly's murder and the find at the church, but they did not give any explanation.

This was to be the last information released by the police until March 2003, when the one-year anniversary of Milly's disappearance was marked by an announcement from the Surrey Constabulary. They declared that there was now a £50,000 reward available to the person that supplied the information that led to the conviction of whoever was responsible for Milly's murder. Surrey Police were putting up £40,000 of the cash and the Crimestoppers Trust the other £10,000. The police described the size of the reward as 'quite exceptional' and said it demonstrated their 'huge commitment' to the case.

Detective Chief Superintendent Denholm placed emphasis on the importance of finding Milly's clothes or the other items she had on her at the time she went missing. He said, 'It would be one of our best opportunities for a breakthrough in this case.' In addition to her school uniform, he said she was wearing a pair of black Pod brand shoes. Her mobile phone was described as a Nokia 3210 with a silver front and blue back. It had 'Milly' marked on it. Her rucksack was now described as beige and black, made by Jansport, and it had contained a small pink 'Barbie' case. She also had a white plastic purse with a red heart on it, and finally he described her house key as being a rim lock and mortise key, which was on a bottle-opener key ring.

The usual police statement count was given as 3,300, and the number of vehicles that had been checked was put at 2,700. Some 500 items had apparently been submitted for forensic examination, and 40 sacks of leaf matter were also being examined. This had been taken from the spot where the remains had been found. Detective Chief Superintendent Denholm declared that he 'remained optimistic' of catching her killer.

Following Milly's disappearance, Bob and Sally Dowler had been particularly anxious about the safety of their elder daughter Gemma. How do you allow your remaining child the freedom that normal teenagers enjoy when you have experienced every parent's worst nightmare? Whenever Gemma went out, Sally would repeatedly phone her in order to find out where she was and what she was doing. When Gemma was with her friends she found these calls embarrassing. Together they found that sending mobile phone text messages was a less obtrusive but equally effective way of keeping in touch, and so they decided to bring this to a wider audience. A charity had already been set up in Milly's memory called 'Milly's Fund', which was established with the aim of promoting personal safety in children and young adults. In October 2003 a campaign was launched, entitled 'Teach UR Mum 2 txt', which for those who do not know translates as 'Teach Your Mum To Text'. Sally, who has since become a devoted safety campaigner, fronted the launch.

Two months later, the Dowlers lent their weight to another scheme, which was being adopted by Surrey Police. This was entitled 'The Child Rescue Alert' and was based on a format already in existence in the United States. When a child is believed to have been abducted, the police and local news agencies come together to put out news flashes across as wide a range of media outlets as possible.

The following year was a relatively quiet one in the media for the Milly Dowler case. Whenever somebody was convicted of a similar crime, the newspapers would suggest he was a suspect and claim that he was to be interviewed in jail, but no major developments or revelations came to light. But 2005 would be entirely different.

On New Year's Eve, as 2005 approached, 22-year-old forensic science student Sally Geeson went out for the night with friends to the Hog's Head pub in Cambridge. She left the pub with a male friend at 1am to get something to eat, but when a fight started outside the takeaway they intended to use her companion stepped in to break it up, and in the ensuing melee they became separated. Sally was unable to find the friends she had previously been with and somehow ended up in a stranger's car. She sent a text message to a friend at 1.40am which read, 'No one waited for me, I have got into a car with someone, please call me.' Two minutes later she sent another message to a male friend saying, 'Please help me x.' Sally was never to be seen alive again, for the car she had got into was being driven by 31-year-old Lance Corporal David Atkinson, a member of the Royal Engineers.

His record of service in the military was disgraceful. He had been disciplined for drunkenness, for disobeying an order, and in 1998 he stood trial at a court martial on charges of kidnapping and false imprisonment. He was acquitted of the kidnapping charge but convicted of the slightly less serious charge of false imprisonment. His victim had been an 18-year-old woman who he had forced into his car and attempted to molest. While awaiting his trial he was held in custody at a military corrective centre for eight months, and the sentencing judge took this into account when sentencing him to what appears to be a ridiculously lenient punishment of a £1,000 fine. Atkinson was based at Waterbeach near Cambridge when he abducted Sally. He had previously been based in Chatham, Kent, and at the Gibraltar Barracks that adjoin Yateley Heath Woods.

Atkinson sexually assaulted Sally and then strangled her. He dumped her body in woodland adjoining an American military cemetery. He then fled to Scotland. The police meanwhile were looking for Sally, and it did not take them long to name

Atkinson as a 'significant person' in their inquiry. Sally's body was eventually found on Friday, 7 January, and news of the discovery was broadcast by the media. Some of her clothes, her handbag and her mobile phone were missing. A few hours later Atkinson set himself on fire and leaped to his death from a seventh-floor hotel window.

A few days later, Surrey Police announced that they were looking into the possibility that he might have been responsible for Milly's death. A spokeswoman said, 'He's not a prime suspect; he's a person of interest. We are liaising with the senior investigating officer in the Geeson murder investigation for information that may be relevant, but also with the Military Police to find out if Atkinson was or could have been in Surrey at the time of Milly's murder.' No further information relating to Atkinson has been forthcoming from Surrey Police.

In March 2005, as the third anniversary of Milly's disappearance loomed, Surrey Police held a media briefing. They announced that they were now looking for a Daewoo Nexia car. This had been seen on CCTV turning left from Copenhagen Way into Station Avenue at 4.33pm on 21 March 2002. This is about 25 minutes after the last positive sighting of Milly. It was pointed out that the vehicle appeared to be low at the rear as if it were heavily laden. Detective Chief Inspector Brian Marjoram, who was now the police voice of the inquiry said, 'We would like to confirm the identity of the owner of the car and find out where it is now. It may well have been used in the abduction of Milly.'

It was also revealed for the first time that Surrey Police were working with Metropolitan Police detectives who were investigating two other murders. In a piece of typically noncommittal and ambiguous police speak, Marjoram said, 'We are liaising closely with the Metropolitan Police team (investigating the murders) and we will keep an open mind about any possible links, although the offences are not formally linked.' The murders he was referring to were those of Marsha McDonnell in February 2003, and that of Amelie Delagrange in August 2004.

Marsha McDonnell was a 19-year-old student returning home from a night out at the cinema with friends. She got off a bus in the suburb of Hampton some five miles from Walton on Thames and was walking home when she was attacked and hit on the head with a blunt instrument, thought to be a hammer. She died from her injuries in hospital. A few weeks earlier a 17-year-old girl had been attacked in the same way in the same area and had survived, although she never fully recovered from her injuries. Soon after the attack on Marsha, an 18-year-old man claimed to have been attacked in a similar manner, although he was later found to be lying and was arrested for wasting police time.

Amelie Delagrange was a 22-year-old French student walking home at night across Twickenham Green some seven miles from where Milly disappeared, when she too was hit on the head with a blunt instrument. The resultant injuries she suffered proved fatal. A number of her possessions were later found in the River Thames at Walton.

A number of other attacks have in turn been linked to these, and it would appear that a serial attacker is on the loose operating in an area close to the scene of Milly's abduction. Should that offender ever be apprehended, it will be interesting to see what transpires in relation to the Milly case, but for now

I prefer to look at her abduction and murder in isolation, in order not to be distracted from what we know.

In May 2005 it was revealed that the Dowler family had been suffering further at the hands of someone who should not have been allowed to enter their lives. Paul Hughes was 36 and a convicted paedophile serving a 56-month prison term for dragging a 12-year-old girl into some bushes and assaulting her. From his cell he wrote a number of disturbing letters to the Dowlers in which he admitted killing Milly. This was impossible as it was proved he was hundreds of miles away at the time she disappeared. All these letters were intercepted by prison staff except for one that was missed and eventually delivered to the family home. It was opened by Milly's sister Gemma, causing much distress. Hughes was charged with attempting to make three threats to kill Gemma, and was sentenced to five years' imprisonment. He will be placed on the sex offenders' register for life.

This merely means that within three days of his release from prison he must attend his local police station and register his new address with them. If he leaves that address for more than seven days, he must register at the police station nearest to where he is staying. But if he has no fixed address upon his release, he can notify the police of which park bench he is sleeping on, as long as the police can find him there. I wish I was joking.

Once again it is time to consider what sort of person may have committed this dreadful crime. I would suggest a person for whom the areas of Walton on Thames and Yateley Heath Woods had some prior and considerable significance. He may have lived, worked or socialised in or near to these places. He may have had relatives or friends nearby who he visited, and therefore got to know his way around. He may have travelled to or through these areas by car, bus or train. I do not believe that Milly was specifically targeted for this attack beforehand. She just had the tragic misfortune to be in the wrong place at the wrong time. For the offender, all prevailing circumstances were right for him to carry out his despicable deed. A suitable victim at a suitable time, in a place where he felt so supremely confident he was able to abduct her.

I believe this person will have come to the attention of the police in some way in the past but not necessarily for a similar type of offence. He will not have lived a perfectly respectable existence before suddenly deciding one day to abduct and murder a child. He may have been a petty criminal or an unpleasant neighbour. He may have inappropriately touched a female before, even perhaps when a child. I would not be surprised if he had been subjected to some form of abuse when young, perhaps psychological, physical or sexual. As a result of this I think he sees himself as a victim, and in this mindset he is able to justify what he does. His excitement at committing this crime may have overcome the caution he would have been expected to show. I believe there would have been a significant change in his behaviour immediately after killing Milly and that he would have returned to his 'normal' pattern of behaviour as time passed and his euphoria subsided.

This person will have a huge sense of his own self-importance. This may not always be readily distinguishable but exists in his head and allows him to overcome the usual feelings people have towards fellow human beings. Do these traits remind you of anyone you know? I'm sure the Surrey Police would like to hear from you if they do.

In any event, this offender was incredibly lucky to have got away with taking a girl in the manner that he did and not get caught. I just hope that in the same way a gambler's lucky streak will inevitably come to an end, so will his.

CHAPTER EIGHT
IT'S WHY WE DO IT

M ick Turner is a big feller. He stands six foot tall and weighs in at 15 stone. I met him for the first time on a gloriously sunny spring day at a motorway service station on the M6. We had spoken a few times before on the phone, and his openness and willingness to speak was a refreshing change from the attitude of many senior police officers I had encountered on my travels.

He has been in the police all his adult life. He joined the Lancashire Constabulary as a 16-year-old cadet in 1972, became a constable in 1975, and soon after decided that CID life, rather than uniform duties, was for him. He has since spent most of his career as a detective, specialising in murder investigations. He has investigated more than a hundred such cases, a staggering number that makes him one of the most experienced homicide cops in the country. If that statistic is not impressive enough, the fact that the crime in this chapter is the only unsolved case on his curriculum vitae is nothing short of remarkable.

His talents and experience have been recognised over the years by his employers, consequently he has risen through the ranks to Detective Superintendent. By the time you read this Mick will have retired from the police, and the people of Lancashire will have lost a fine public servant.

We shook hands and I noticed he was wearing his crime scene accreditation badge around his neck. I felt strangely reassured and was immediately impressed by his calm air of professionalism and easygoing manner.

I followed his car and we soon headed south down the A49 towards a village called Charnock Richard. The housing here is spread out; it feels as though there is plenty of space and a local estate agent boasts that 'it has something for everyone'. We drove into a road called Back Lane past pretty cottages, large detached and smaller semi-detached houses, farm buildings and open fields – very nice if that's what takes your fancy. We passed over the M6 and were now just to the west of the motorway. We came to a track running off Back Lane, which was on our right. I noticed a small area at the end of the track was covered with tarmac, and this is where Mick and I parked.

During one of our earlier telephone conversations Mick had told me to bring my Wellington boots with me. I had been too embarrassed to tell him I did not own any, so as he donned his well-worn pair I took my brand spanking-new ones out of my carrier bag. When I had tried them on in the shop they had fitted perfectly, but when it came to getting them off I had needed the assistance of my wife. I was now terrified that the same might happen again, and that I would have to call on Mick for help when we had finished looking at the scene. I shouldn't think a man of his position was too used to helping people in such a way, so I just burbled something to him about these being my first ever pair and he looked at me in utter disbelief.

We walked down this track, the tarmac soon came to an end and thereafter it was mainly mud but wide enough for a car or farm vehicle. A hundred metres down the track we went through a farm gate and on all sides we were surrounded by farmland.

I saw a large pipe running alongside the track and Mick explained that it carried excess rainwater from cultivated fields down into a small pond. It was a large pipe and 30 years ago when I was a slim teenager I reckon I could have crawled into it. Subsequent excesses and the resultant middle-age spread would make that impossible today.

In July 2002, a lady walking her dog had noticed what she thought were bones partially submerged in the pond at the end of this pipe. She was not really convinced of what she had seen, and had taken advice from members of her family before finally calling the police on Friday, 26 July. Uniformed officers attended, soon followed by Mick. He was sure these were human bones, but as a lot of animal bones are discovered in these parts a bone was taken and rushed to the home of a pathologist. A swift analysis confirmed they were human remains. Among the many specialists called to the scene by Mick was a forensic archaeologist from the University of Central Lancashire. This type of archaeologist specialises in recovering bodies without losing evidence, a vitally important expert for this type of case.

In order to properly examine the remains as they lay, and to thoroughly search the bottom of the pond for any other evidence, the police underwater search team was called in to drain it. The pond at the time was about two feet deep in the middle and slightly shallower at the edges. It is about five paces wide and almost circular, so there was a significant amount of water to remove, which was done using an electric pump. Once the water had been pumped out, a human skeleton was clearly visible and was described by experts as being in 'archeological order'. That is to say it was almost complete and laying with the bones in their correct order and position. Only the left hand, the kneecaps and two pieces of skull were missing.

The fact the remains were submerged and that a hand was missing brought back memories of a previous murder that had occurred in these parts back in 1979. Two amateur scuba divers had found a body weighed down with rocks on a ledge some ten metres deep in a flooded quarry called Eccleston Delph, in Heskin. This is less than a mile from Charnock Richard. When the corpse was brought to the surface, it was discovered that both hands had been chopped off in an effort to conceal its identity.

It turned out to be the body of Marty Johnstone, a New Zealander who worked for one of the world's most notorious drug barons of the time, Terence Alexander Sinclair. Sinclair was a fellow Kiwi who had progressed from lesser crimes such as burglary into worldwide drug distribution. He managed his empire with ruthless efficiency and during the 1970s he had ordered at least ten murders, possibly many more, in various countries including Australia, New Zealand and France. The victims were usually drug mules who had cooperated with the authorities. They were usually shot, and on one occasion a woman who was an intended target was walking with her six-year-old daughter when a hitman pounced. Neither of them were spared.

Sinclair moved to the UK under one of many aliases as the heat from law enforcement agencies in the Antipodes became too much to bear. With easy access to the £50m he had acquired through his crimes, and which he had managed to conceal from the authorities, he did not have any trouble integrating into British society.

Johnstone had made the foolish error of attempting to double-cross Sinclair over a deal, so another member of the syndicate, Andy Maher, was tasked with killing him. Maher shot him, hacked off his hands and deposited him in the quarry.

Lancashire Police launched their murder inquiry, which mushroomed in size as they tried to unravel Sinclair's vast empire. He was arrested in London and later stood trial with Maher and a number of others. Over 130 witnesses from around the world gave evidence, many of whom live under aliases to this day. Sinclair and Maher both received 20-year sentences. Sinclair died of a heart attack in Parkhurst prison in 1983, having served only a fraction of his sentence. On hearing this, officers from Lancashire went to the prison to examine his corpse, as they feared a body might have been supplanted and that he might have escaped. They were relieved to find this was not the case and that Sinclair, who by now was only in his mid-40s, was indeed dead.

In Charnock Richard, we stood over the pond staring at the spot where the skeleton of this latest submerged victim had been found. Mick said, 'When I looked at these remains I was convinced that we would find out who that person was. Not for one moment did I contemplate that we would not establish that person's identity.'

A Home Office pathologist attended the scene and conducted a thorough post-mortem at the mortuary later. A forensic scientist and a biologist also visited although there was little for them to do, as it was clear the body had been in the pond for some considerable time and the normal evidence associated with murder scenes was not present.

There were no clothes or shoes on the body, nor were any found nearby. Had the victim been wearing shoes when put in the pond, they would have deteriorated at a much slower rate than the body and would almost certainly have been discovered. No weapons were found.

A camera was placed into the drainage pipe that relayed images of the entire length of the inside, but nothing of interest was seen. I asked Mick if he thought the body might have originally been secreted in it. He said that while that might have been a possibility, it was considered extremely unlikely as the bones would have been washed out bit by bit and found in a haphazard arrangement as opposed to 'in archeological order'.

As only bones could be seen – there was no flesh or organs – it was clear decomposition was virtually complete. A body goes through different stages of decomposition after death and, by identifying what stage it is in, it is sometimes possible to establish time of death. Firstly there is 'initial decay', when the body can look almost like it did when alive, but, because of bacteria and other enzymes that are in a body when it is alive, decomposition starts. Next there is 'putrefaction', when organisms in the body begin to make it swell and smell. 'Black putrefaction' happens next when the flesh begins to turn black or in fact blue, green, purple or brown. Gases now begin to escape from the corpse and the smell is horrendous.

Members of the public questioned near to the scene did recall a bad smell from the area, but were unable to pinpoint when. It is also common for farm animals to be killed by predators or to otherwise die in rural areas such as this, and they of course give off a bad smell when decaying. The next part of bodily breakdown is called 'butyric fermentation', when the tissues and organs turn to fluid and in this case may have been washed away. A small stream runs off the pond to the left of the drainage pipe, so there is a constant flow of water through the pond, and it is thought much of the remains may have disappeared down this route. It is also believed this corpse suffered the indignity of having parts of it devoured by foxes and other wild animals.

Finally, the body decays further when tissue rots and shrinks, leaving only the skeleton. On these remains only a tiny amount of body tissue was found attached to bones. When examination of the scene was complete, under the supervision of the forensic archaeologist, undertakers carefully removed the bones. They were taken to the local mortuary.

After this the pond was dredged by the Underwater Search Unit, and the silt was taken away for examination by archaeologists. Not one microscopic trace of evidence was found. No fragments of human remains, nor clothing, jewellery or other personal effects. Not only was this a blow to the murder squad, it was a clear indication that the body had been naked when put in the water, and it meant almost certainly that this person died elsewhere.

The post-mortem began. Mick and the archaeologist were

present. The remains presented a huge challenge to the pathologist, not only to try to establish cause of death, but to do all that could be done in order to find this person's identity. Mick also had to confirm that this death was indeed murder and not some sort of misadventure, say an accident or a suicide.

Two massive skull fractures were thought to be the cause of death. Without the evidence to be certain, the pathologist described this cause as 'highly likely'. It could have been that the victim was strangled, for example, and then had his head bashed in, but either way accident was ruled out, as these fractures were believed to have been inflicted with a blunt instrument. Having established that the case was indeed a murder, all attention was now focused on finding out who the victim was.

Mick began by setting 'parameters' in order to establish who the victim was not. Firstly the post-mortem revealed that the victim was male. The skeleton was that of an adult, so missing children would not be considered. Next he wanted to establish the victim's height, which was put at between five-foot six and five-foot eight, so all persons substantially taller or shorter than this could be discounted.

It was also noted that this person was of unusually small stature, which suggested that he might be of Asian descent. A blow was dealt to the inquiry when the teeth were found to be unimproved. There had been no fillings, no crowns fitted or anything similar, so it was unlikely that a dental record for him would be traced. Mick said, 'It was at this point that I feared for the first time that fate may not be on our side.'

Apart from the skull fractures, no other bone injuries were found, again not good news for the investigating team. If there had been evidence of a previous break of a limb then medical records might have yielded some clues to his identity. This was also an indicator that the body had not been stripped of its tissue and organs prior to being put in the pond, as any such butchery might well have left marks on the bones. The archaeologist did, however, form the opinion that the victim might have walked with a limp, as he noticed a minor abnormality in one of the hips.

A sample of ground-down bone was taken from one of the heel bones in order to establish a DNA profile. The sample was submitted to the Forensic Science Service, which operates and administers the National DNA Database (NDNAD) on behalf of the Association of Chief Police Officers. The NDNAD contains profiles of nearly 3,000,000 people in the UK, and another 40,000 are added each month. These profiles are obtained when people are arrested and subjected to a mouth swab. Since April 2004, when new legislation came into force, the police are now empowered to take a DNA sample from any person arrested for any offence that is punishable with a term of imprisonment. Even if a person is merely questioned after arrest and not charged, their DNA can be taken and stored on the database. This has angered many civil libertarians who believe a sample should only be stored if a person is convicted. I think they have a fair point. Imagine for example that a neighbour who you do not get on with makes a spurious allegation against you of assault or threatening behaviour. The police arrive and arrest you, and once at the police station they compel you to supply a DNA sample. The allegation is found out to be untrue, in fact downright malicious, but once you are released the state is in possession of your entire genetic make-up. Something that has not been shown to have happened yet, but surely will one day, will be DNA evidence being found to have been planted by some wayward servant of Her Majesty.

I understand that the NDNAD is a mighty tool for the police. It helps them catch about twenty-five murderers and sixty rapists a month, along with thousands of car thieves and burglars. I would not like to see its use severely restricted, but I do think that mere arrest is far too flimsy a reason for samples to be taken.

The post-mortem could not assist much more, but a lot of other expertise was to be called upon. The parameters Mick set remained wide at that stage; it still had not been established when the victim had died, but Mick was a firm believer in utilising the press, so information was released as it was deemed appropriate. The media latched on to the fact the victim might have had a limp, and made much of it in their articles. Mick called upon a doctor of podiatry – a specialist in feet and how people walk. Mick wanted to investigate the hip abnormality thoroughly. The doctor's opinion was that, while the victim might have had some kind of genetic hip defect, there was no evidence to suggest he would have walked with a limp. This was a frustrating time for Mick, as by now the press had got the public concentrating on a limp that might not have existed.

Officers were tasked with examining missing person files held on the Police National Computer (PNC). These records were often found to be unreliable, as insufficient care had been taken by those compiling them. Missing person inquiries are often not at the top of the pile when it comes to policing priorities, unless of course it is a child, and apparently it showed in these poorly compiled files.

As a result of this, a charity organisation, the National Missing

Persons Helpline (NMPH), was consulted. The NMPH was established in 1992 by two women, Janet Newman and Mary Asprey. They defined the purpose of the charity as 'to advise and support people who go missing, and to help those who the missing leave behind'. They give priority to the young and the old, the sick and the vulnerable, but they also maintain the largest database in the country of all missing people. This is a substantial task. The Home Office estimates that 200,000 people go missing in the UK each year. Most of them return unharmed within three days, however many thousands do not.

The NMPH does magnificent work in supporting and tracing juvenile runaways, reuniting families, as well as staffing their various telephone helplines. Over the years, members of staff have developed expertise in forensic artistry, facial reconstruction, the identification of skeletal remains, and much more. Some of the victims of Fred and Rosemary West were identified from records held by the NMPH.

Males in their late 20s are the group of adults most likely to go missing. Consequently, NMPH have quite a number on their database. Hopes of a match were high, but none was found. It was a disappointment for the investigators, but Mick was keen to go on record as saying how professional and helpful the NMPH had been.

The media campaign, however, was generating results. Literally hundreds of possible names were being put forward. Those that were obviously not the victim were filtered out manually by murder squad staff, while other suggested names, and there were over 700 of them, were 'actioned' for detectives to investigate.

Next the bones were taken on another journey, this time to

the University of Glasgow, where two departments were asked to help. Firstly the skull was examined by the Facial Reconstruction Unit, who set about making a computer-generated image of how the victim's face might have looked. This is done by laying photographic images over one another, eventually building up a possible facial likeness.

The next expert to assist was Professor Susan Black OBE, BSc, PhD, a consultant forensic anthropologist in the Human Identification Unit at the University of Glasgow. She has a doctorate in human anatomy and over 25 years' experience in her field. Professor Black has helped the FBI and various foreign governments over the years and was honoured by the Queen with an OBE for her sterling work, such as identifying victims in Kosovo.

Mick gave her a box that by now contained jumbled up bones. Within minutes she had the skeleton laid out in perfect order, and began to give forth her views. She was able to be far more precise than any previous opinion. She confirmed the victim was male, and also his height. She described his build as 'gracile', a word so uncommon my computer does not even recognise it, which means slight, extremely so, of almost feminine proportions. She confirmed there was indeed evidence of hip displacement, but that the victim had compensated for this in his walk. Mick was becoming more and more impressed as the examination went on.

Professor Black said the Asian subcontinent was where the victim's 'gene pool', or ancestors, had most likely originated. She put the probability of this at 90 per cent. He was described as being in his third decade, therefore aged between 20 and 30. Professor Black was able to pinpoint this by examining the shape and fusion of some of the bones. Various bones do not become fully fused until people are over 20 years old. The missing bones on his left hand were explained by the evidence of animal scraping. Four teeth had been removed by way of dentistry, possibly in his childhood, in order to make room in his narrow palate. Even so, the remaining teeth were still crowded. Another four were missing and had been removed after death, either washed away or taken by an animal. The remaining teeth were described as being in excellent condition, which indicated a strong presence of fluoride in his diet, or a diet with few sugar based foods.

From the tiny amount of soft tissue that remained on the bones and from the appearance of the skull, the surface of which had the texture of the skin of a orange, she was able to say that the victim suffered from iron deficiency anaemia. This is a condition in which a person's blood cannot carry enough oxygen. This may be due to a lack of red blood cells, or due to a lack of the chemical haemoglobin. The condition may also arise if a person loses blood quicker than the body can replace it. A person may not know they are losing blood as it may be passed in their stools. I make no apology for the following list of the causes and the symptoms of this condition, which are many, because while this condition is by no means rare it may provide vital clues as we try to identify this man.

CAUSES OF IRON DEFICIENCY ANAEMIA
- Stomach ulcers, piles, inflammation of the colon or bowel cancer, which can cause internal bleeding
- Kidney or bladder disease, which may cause the blood to be passed in urine

- Chronic diarrhoea, or gluten sensitivity
- Lack of iron in diet, although this is unlikely to be the cause in an adult living in the UK
- Cancer or rheumatoid arthritis
- Long-term aspirin use
- Hookworm infection – this can occur in people who have travelled to tropical countries

SYMPTOMS OF IRON DEFICIENCY ANAEMIA

- Breathlessness
- Tiredness
- Dizziness
- Rapid or weak pulse, palpitations
- Headaches
- Pale skin
- Brittle nails
- Cracked lips
- Inflamed or smooth tongue
- A burning sensation in the tongue
- Dryness in the mouth and throat
- Brittle hair
- Difficulty in swallowing
- Occasionally people develop 'pica', a craving for a particular type of food, liquorice for example, or for a non-food consumable like ice

Armed with this new information and the computer-generated facial image, Mick went to the press once again. Still no one came forward with the identity of the victim, so the Unit of Art and Medicine at Manchester University were now brought on board to assist. They specialise in forensic facial construction, and although Mick already had a facial image that had been made by the University of Glasgow it was a sign of his dogged determination to solve this case that once again he sought more expertise. This reconstruction was to take the form of a life-size clay model of the victim's head. This Manchester University unit had been established in the 1970s under the leadership of one of the pioneers in this field, Richard Neave. He was the mentor of the lady who now heads the unit, Dr Caroline Wilkinson.

She set about making a clay model of how she believed the victim's head, face and neck would have looked. Mick revealed the completed model to the press at a briefing on Tuesday, 22 October 2002. I remembered seeing this on television, and recalled how I was taken aback by the distinctive image. I wanted to know more about how this model had been made, so I asked for an appointment with Dr Wilkinson and she was kind enough to spare me some of her valuable time.

She has worked in the unit since 1995, during which time she has obtained a doctorate in facial anthropology. She has been the head of the unit since 2000 when Richard Neave retired. Most of the unit's work is in relation to archaeology for museums. They have reconstructed faces of ancient Egyptians, Robert the Bruce, Philip II of Macedon, and those of many other unidentified people. Through this work much useful historical information has been learned. But the real reason for the unit's existence is its forensic work and its assistance to murder and missing persons inquiries. This may form only a small part of their workload, but as Dr Wilkinson said to me, 'It's why we do it.'

The unit rightfully takes pride in the cases in which they have had much success. An example of this was the discovery of a badly decomposed body found wrapped in a piece of old carpet and buried in the garden of a derelict house in Wales. This unpleasant find was made by builders carrying out excavation work. The facial reconstruction made by the Manchester unit was so accurate that when it was shown to the public the response was astonishing. Local 15-year-old girl Karen Price had gone missing in 1981, and on seeing the clay model many people suggested it looked like her. This led to other forensic tests being performed that confirmed it was indeed that unfortunate girl. Two men were later convicted of offences relating to her murder.

The reputation of the unit spreads further than the UK. In 2001, the people of the Netherlands were shocked by the discovery of the dismembered remains of a four-year-old girl. Body parts were found across the country, including a decomposed and severed head on a beach in Nulde. As a result of this the case became known as 'the girl from Nulde'. Again the Manchester unit made a reconstruction that when released to the public led to the child's identification, and once again murder convictions followed.

The first stage of the process of this reconstruction, called 'the Manchester method', is to take a plaster cast of the skull. Dr Wilkinson commented that this victim had a particularly small head. The skull is then mounted on a pole, and the jawbone is attached. The teeth are added, and the jaw is set so that the mouth is in a relaxed position as it would be in a living person. The thickness of facial tissue, muscles and skin will be dictated by the sex, age and ethnic origin of the person. In order to gauge this correctly, small holes are drilled into the cast of the skull, into which wooden pegs of the correct length are inserted. These will act as guides when the facial tissue is replicated.

Plaster or plastic eyes are then inserted in the position dictated by the orbital bones. Next the muscles of the neck and face are added. These are built up in layers according to the shape of the skull. There are hundreds of muscles in a face, around the eyes, mouth, nose, ears, forehead and chin, together with a number of glands that are also added. Finally the layer of clay representing the skin is sculpted.

In some cases hair is added if information from scenes of crime officers or forensic anthropologists can give some indication as to what it may have looked like. This was not possible in this case, as only a microscopic trace of a hairline was evident on the skull. Unless specifically asked to be speculative about any features, Dr Wilkinson will only add features of which she can be certain.

Mick did ask her to add hair and skin colour to photographs of the reconstruction later. This was done using computer software. Now, exclusively for the first time, I have been granted permission by Mick to release these images to the public. They have not previously been published as the additions were somewhat speculative, and it was feared that they, like the limp issue, might serve only to encourage the public to consider people who looked exactly like the images. But as more than three years have passed since the discovery of the remains and there is still no positive identification it has been decided that their release may now help.

The entire process of constructing the clay model took only two days, a remarkably short time. This procedure is dictated by science and by the vast amount of information that is noticeable only to the expert from the examination of the skull. The great skill of Dr Wilkinson is the way she combines her scientific knowledge with her interpretation of the data through her artistic talents to come up with the finished article. For anybody who wants to know more about this subject, may I recommend Dr Wilkinson's authoritative book *Forensic Facial Reconstruction*.

Now look at the features of the reconstruction that stand out. The shape and size of a nose is dictated by the nasal spine. In this case the distinctive nose is long, downward sloping and asymmetrical, in that it slopes to the right. Of all these factors we can be confident as to the accuracy. The only part that has been guesstimated is the tip, as nose tips are fleshy and not dictated by bone structure.

His bottom lip protrudes slightly – Dr Wilkinson was able to be confident of this – as this happens when teeth meet flush, and his did. As a further consequence of this he has a distinctive chin.

After the model was shown to the public, hopes among the murder squad were raised significantly when five people from the Southampton area called the incident room. They each gave the same name of a man who they thought the victim could be. Officers were dispatched immediately to find out more but they found the man alive and well. At least he could be eliminated from the inquiry!

When I was in the force there was a saying that was used to describe a detective who pursued a case relentlessly and was a formidable adversary to anybody he arrested. The saying was 'I wouldn't want to be nicked by him'. I think this applies to Mick Turner. Undaunted, he pressed on. This was a man unaccustomed to not solving murders.

The next expert to be called upon was Professor Ken Pye, a forensic geologist, who was recommended to Mick by the National Crime and Operations Faculty (NCOF). The NCOF is part of the National Centre for Policing Expertise (CENTREX), which is based in Hampshire. These faculties provide a huge range of expertise and knowledge to their colleagues over a wide range of policing issues. As well as providing specialist expertise, the NCOF analyses serious crime, can manage incidents if need be, and can provide numerous other forms of support to an operation. The NCOF has earned itself a worthy worldwide reputation.

Professor Pye has developed techniques that enable him to examine 'trace elements' or 'chemical signatures', which are deposits found in bones. These deposits vary according to whatever a person has consumed during their lifetime. This includes food, water, even the air that they breathe. Somebody living in a city will have breathed more lead than a country dweller, and this will show in their bones. Some people who lived in parts of the north-west of England at the time of the Chernobyl disaster will have traces of the radioactive gases that blew over that part of the UK, whereas someone from the South, which was unaffected, will not. These types of factors will help pinpoint where a person may have lived. Professor Pye is also able to give an indication as to when a person may have died.

His work came to prominence when he examined the torso of a boy found floating in the River Thames in September 2001. The boy was aged between five and seven years old. His head, arms and legs had been expertly severed and the torso was naked except for a pair of orange shorts. Forensic examination revealed that shortly before death he had consumed a potion containing quartz, animal bone, clay and rough gold. This led detectives to believe he had been the victim of a sacrificial or 'muti' killing, most often practised in parts of Africa.

Professor Pye examined the bones of the child victim and found traces of a particular type of rock found in parts of West Africa. Officers travelled to Nigeria and took samples from rock, soil, wild animals and human post-mortems over a 10,000-kilometre area. By comparing these samples to the traces in the bones of the torso, Professor Pye was able to pinpoint a small area of Nigeria from where the boy must have originated. Unfortunately, no person has yet been convicted of that crime.

In the Charnock Richard case he estimated that the victim had been dead for 15 months, give or take three months either way. This put the time of his murder between October 2000 and June 2001. He also stated the victim had lived in the UK for most, if not all, of his life. Mick was delighted to hear this. The inquiry was reinvigorated by the news as they felt it increased their chances of a positive identification. Professor Pye also deduced from deposits left by drinking water that this person was quite likely to have lived in or near a large conurbation north-west of Birmingham, possibly Wolverhampton, for at least the last ten years.

When this information was coupled with the 90 per cent certainty that he was of Asian descent, it was decided to print appeal posters in no less than ten different languages. These included Urdu, Punjabi, Hindi and Gujarati. They were then circulated to police forces around the country that had significant Asian communities living within their boundaries. Mick and his team targeted the West Midlands area. A press conference was arranged and another incident room set up in

Wolverhampton. It was the beginning of 2003, and a new year brought renewed optimism that this was a case they were going to get to the bottom of.

Unfortunately a gang of machine-gun-wielding thugs reduced press attention in Mick's case considerably. At about 4am on 2 January, 18-year-old Charlene Ellis and 17-year-old Letisha Shakespeare were gunned down and killed as they stood outside a hairdressing salon in Aston, Birmingham. They were getting some fresh air, a change from the stifling heat of the party going on inside. Two other girls were seriously wounded and the West Midlands Police launched a huge inquiry. National media covered the case with considerable interest.

Consequently Mick's case had a lot of competition for press attention. In any event he went ahead with his press briefing. About thirty journalists attended, which was a reasonable number considering the more 'newsworthy' events that had occurred nearby.

A promising lead arose when the clay model was said to resemble an Asian man known as 'Sunny', who had previously lived in the Wolverhampton area but had not been seen for about ten years. Sunny had been known to frequent various pubs and also to use a variety of different names. He was believed to be a Hindu originating from the Punjab and had arrived in the UK in 1991 having previously applied for asylum in Germany. 'Sunny', however, was later traced living in India.

A reasonable theory that the team applied some thought to was that their victim might have been the subject of an 'honour killing'. These types of murders are mainly prevalent in Muslim countries, and occur when a family member is perceived to have brought shame upon a family name. Women are more commonly the victims and are killed for such 'crimes' as dating someone from a different religion or creed, or running away from an arranged marriage. These killings have occurred in France and Turkey recently and are an ever-increasing problem in the UK.

Men have been the intended victims of such murders in Britain, and one example was that of 26-year-old Abdullah Yasin. He married the daughter of 49-year-old Mohammed Arshad, a man previously regarded as a pillar of society, who had served as a justice of the peace and also on the Tayside Racial Equality Council. Yasin came from a different caste, which was unacceptable to Arshad, who tried to hire a hitman to kill him. Fortunately for Yasin, Arshad was arrested and later convicted.

Another theory suggested was that the victim might have been involved in organised crime and might have been killed by fellow gangsters in a scenario similar to that of Marty Johnstone. Sources in the underworld were contacted, but to no avail. Until his identity is discovered, these will remain just theories.

Fourteen months had passed since the discovery of the remains when Mick decided to take his appeal for information to India. The test cricketer Virender Sehwag offered his services and made a taped appeal that was widely broadcast in the subcontinent.

Returning home empty-handed, and with no other obvious avenues to explore, it was decided that the case would now lie dormant. Mick still feels a huge sense of professional disappointment and frustration. 'We should have been able to sort this out, but when it came to identifying him we didn't get past first base.' The incident room was shut down and a closing report compiled. If the case remains unsolved, every two years the file will be examined and an assessment of Mick's investigation will take place. If, however, any fresh information comes to light, the case will immediately be reopened and a thorough investigation of that information will take place.

I have given much thought as to how I could take this case forward, apart from including it in this book. I wondered if it would be possible to send an email containing both the images of the facial reconstructions and the information we have found out about this victim to everybody in my contacts list. I thought that if they in turn then forwarded it on in the same fashion we might establish the global electronic equivalent of an old style chain letter. This may reach a far wider audience and increase the chances of solving this crime. I spoke to Mick about this and he was very keen on the idea. He spoke to the officer who has recently taken over his position following his retirement, and as a result I am currently working with the Lancashire Constabulary on the development of a suitable computer program. All of us working on the project are very excited about other possible applications this software might have, not only in crime detection but also in issues of public safety. If you would like to partake in this pioneering crime-fighting scheme, send an email entitled 'clues' to bleksley@gmail.com . You may also use this address for any other communication with me.

I will now list all that we know about this victim. Not every piece of information may be totally accurate, but if you find yourself recognising a few of the features or if any of the reconstruction images remind you in some way of someone you have not seen for some time, then please forward me your suggestions and I will pass them on to the Lancashire Constabulary.

Male, 20 to 30 years old
More than likely of Asian origin (10 per cent chance he was not)
Between five-foot six and five-foot eight tall
Very slim build, almost feminine, with a particularly small head
Genetic hip defect that may have affected his walk
Excellent condition teeth, although he had a crowded and narrow palate
Four teeth removed, probably in childhood
Suffered from iron deficiency anaemia
Distinctive and long sloping nose
Bottom lip that protruded slightly
Distinctive chin
Lived in the UK most, if not all, of his life
May have lived in Wolverhampton or elsewhere near to Birmingham
May have been killed between October 2000 and June 2001

I still find it strange that over three years after the discovery of his remains and over four years since his death, nobody has come forward with a name. People of course go missing every day of the week, but they are normally reported as such. Surely someone somewhere is missing a son, husband, uncle, nephew, cousin or friend.

Whoever this victim was, and whatever he may have done in his life, one thing we know is that he suffered hugely, not only in the manner he was killed but in the undignified way his corpse was discarded and left to rot. People deal with their Christmas turkey carcass in a more appropriate way.

On 18 January 2005, he was buried and finally afforded some dignity. B Livesey Ltd, a firm of funeral directors from Chorley, a town near to where he was found, provided an oak veneer coffin and their services free of charge. The local council footed the bill for the burial site at the cemetery. Local rector John Cree officiated and conducted a service incorporating elements of many differing faiths. Ken Mayler, a coroner's officer from the Lancashire Constabulary, was present, and together with staff from the undertakers and the cemetery, there were a total of seven mourners. Chris Livesey from the funeral directors took photographs, in order that a permanent reminder of this occasion would be available for any relatives if they were found. A brass plaque on the coffin read 'Unknown male, died 26.7.2002, at rest'.

CHAPTER NINE

MAD WORLD

I have had the privilege of meeting many brave people in my life. They include numerous cops, personnel who have seen active service, children who have fought illness and disability, and a close friend who is currently battling cancer with such courage and dignity that I am humbled whenever I am in her company. A man who I consider to be right up there with my personal heroes is Dr Alan Aylward. On each and every occasion that we have met and spoken, I have been struck by his dignity and resolve in the face of suffering incalculable grief, for in the early hours of Saturday, 12 May 2001, as millions of football fans slept soundly, anticipating the FA Cup final that was to take place later that day, his eldest son Jan was murdered by gun-toting hoodlums in Streatham, south London.

Jan, who was 27 years old, had spent the evening at a friend's house in nearby West Norwood High Street. Both he and his friend were fanatical about their cars and their in-car sound systems. A car manufacturer's standard stereo would never do for Jan; he wanted a customised, one-off, homemade and unique system capable of emitting so many decibels that it could burst your eardrums. That is if you were foolish enough to crank it up to its maximum output. This took some achieving. Jan studied the science of sound whenever he could, often using the internet, and was forever modifying or otherwise tinkering with his system. Such was his devotion to his hobby that he removed the rear seats from his distinctive black BMW in order to make room for some huge speakers and the other necessary equipment that accompanied them. This mass of technology did not come cheap, and in order to conceal it from prying eyes he had the windows of his car tinted black. The front windscreen was also tinted, albeit in a slightly lighter shade of grey. Jan had lowered the suspension of the car until it almost hugged the road, and had added snazzy alloy wheels. The end product was an eye-catching mobile music machine of which he was immensely proud.

The journey from his friend's house to the home he shared with his dad, stepmother and younger brother in Valleyfield Road, Streatham, was less than two miles and should have taken only a few minutes. He could have gone an even shorter route but, as his car was so low to the road, Jan preferred roads where he would not encounter speed bumps and run the risk of bottoming out his beloved machine. Consequently he used to stick to main roads wherever possible.

His car turned into Valleyfield Road, and his father told me his recollection of the events that followed in an interview. 'Jan went out with some friends after work,' he said. 'He had been working in the shop [Jan worked as a manager in a pet shop in nearby Streatham Vale. This business had been purchased with financial assistance from his dad]. It was a Friday night. We went to bed early that night. I was woken up early in the morning, about two o'clock, by this rat-a-tat-a-tat sound coming from up the road. I woke up thinking that sounded like shots. But I thought, That's stupid, we live in a decent area of Streatham, it must be something else that made that sound. I thought, Who the hell is making a noise at this time of night? This was followed by the noise of a racing engine, a rrrm rrrm rrrm. I thought it was someone backing up the hill or something. But then it kept going at the same sort of volume and from the same place. Eventually that noise got cut off and I half drifted back to sleep. I was thinking about where Jan was, as I knew he wasn't home yet. I thought he'd be back soon and went off to sleep.

'The next thing I knew there where flashing lights outside, lots of noise and disturbance, so I looked out of the window. There was a fire engine up the road and a police car outside our house blocking the road off. But I couldn't see what was going on; it was obviously something up the road, and I thought it was nothing to do with us, why should it be? But at the same time I was wondering where Jan was. He wasn't back yet. My other son was woken by all of this. He looked out of the window and then went outside to find out what was happening. He came back and said it was something to do with a car up the road, and so we both went and spoke to the police outside. They told us there had been a shooting, and we saw someone pointing at our house and wondered what that meant. My son told the policeman that Jan hadn't come back yet and he asked us what sort of car Jan drove. We told him it was a BMW and he seemed very interested. He asked us if we would go and see the car that was out there. We got dressed and walked up towards where all the police cars were. It was only about a hundred and fifty yards from our house. Sure enough, it was Jan's car.'

Fighting back the emotions, Alan paused for a while before continuing. 'It had driven into the little front garden of a house on the other side of the road. It had gone up the pavement, smashed through the garden wall and was by the front door of this house. I thought, What the hell is going on? I couldn't understand what was happening, but I immediately knew there was something seriously wrong because the policeman I was talking to got on his radio and said, "Yes, I've got the next of kin here." They didn't say much more other than there had been a shooting, and they drove me down to the hospital.'

Alan bravely continued with the interview, showing incredible resolve, which I guessed had helped him considerably in the past four years. 'Essentially, Jan was dead. He was breathing, half-choking from some stuff in the back of his throat; his body was going, but the doctor said he'd been shot through the head and there wasn't any chance. He was dead anyway and they were just keeping the body alive.'

Jan was declared dead at 4.30am. A post-mortem was arranged for 8am at Greenwich mortuary. Alan went on, 'Bullet holes were found in the car and shells on the ground. He was shot through the side of the head; he hadn't even looked round to see who it was. We don't even know why he died. He had been out to his friend's and was driving back. Did those who did it take umbrage at something that he did, or did they mistake him for somebody else? I'd seen a car very similar to his driving around, I told the police. In fact it was so similar that I had mistaken it for his before, and I joked with him about not driving around in a car like that, that it looked like a pimp or a gangster's car. It was ludicrous because he didn't have the kind of lifestyle that you'd expect someone to have driving a car like that. It was so low to the ground that he drove it very carefully.'

A Murder Investigation Team (MIT) from the Metropolitan Police was to conduct the inquiry. They held their first press conference on 18 May 2001. The officer in charge of the investigation Detective Chief Inspector Ken Pandolfi addressed the media. 'Jan was callously murdered on his way home in a cowardly attack that has left his family completely devastated' 'We need to hear from anyone who was in the vicinity of Valleyfield Road at the time who may have seen or heard anything suspicious or who may have seen his distinctive car. We are keeping an open mind about the possible motive at this time.'

Alan was introduced to the media, who were informed of his occupation as head of the Atmospheric Physics Laboratory at a renowned London university. Alan described Jan to the press. 'He was quiet, bright and rather shy. He put all his energy into his work and hobby. He was a harmless son, and we can't work out why anybody would want to kill him.'

The police were soon working on three lines of inquiry. This I have discovered from DCI Nick Scala, an officer who was involved in the investigation from the outset and who now heads up the hunt for Jan's killers. He agreed to speak to me following a request to do so from Alan Aylward. The first theory was that Jan might have been involved in some sort of illegal activity that resulted in his murder. To this end they obtained the keys to his pet shop, Oliver's Pet Supplies, from Alan, and they then went through it with a fine-tooth comb. Both the premises and the accounts were subjected to rigorous scrutiny. The task of examining the books was made easier for them because Jan had been extremely particular about keeping them in order. His younger brother was upset by this police intrusion; he was grieving and could not understand why this was necessary, but he was placated by his father who pragmatically accepted the reasons why the police were taking this course of action. It turned up nothing. Every inquiry they conducted into Jan brought them to the same conclusion: that he was the decent, hard-working, lovable young man everybody knew him to be.

The second line of inquiry was that he might have been involved in some sort of road-rage incident that had escalated dramatically and resulted in the shooting. To this end all CCTV from the area between West Norwood and Streatham, and beyond, was seized. Petrol stations, housing estates, takeaway food outlets – anywhere with CCTV cameras – had their tapes seized.

The last possibility considered was that Jan might have been the victim of mistaken identity. As it was not possible to see into his car, it was felt that it might have been mistaken for a similar one that was connected to some sort of nefarious activity. The Murder Investigation Team carried on with their meticulous work.

Meanwhile, on Tuesday, 29 May, two black brothers Cyrus and David Moses were looking for a place to park outside the Atlantis Night Club, Purley Way, Croydon, in Surrey, which is some six miles from Streatham. They tried to get into an unoccupied space but found their route blocked by two vehicles, one of which was a seven series BMW. An effort by the Moses brothers to request that these vehicles move was greeted by one of the occupants of the BMW getting out and brandishing a sub-machine-gun. The gunman, who was also black, then fired a number of shots into the air before making his way over to Cyrus, who by now was trying to take cover. As he scrambled away the gunman walked up to him and shot him in the leg. The noise of the gunshots alerted members of the public who called the police.

The police arrived at the scene and gave life-saving first aid to Cyrus and circulated to their colleagues some descriptions of the vehicles involved, including the registration number of the seven series BMW: J11 HSK. It was soon spotted and a chase followed that was later described in court as being 'straight from a Hollywood film'. The BMW was pursued at terrifying speed through the streets of south London. A police van involved in the chase was hit by one of many bullets fired at it. Other police vehicles were also shot at. In their desperation to escape, the occupants of the BMW openly fired weapons including an Uzi sub-machine-gun indiscriminately at the police. Miraculously no members of the public or police were hit.

The chase came to an end when the BMW crashed in Thornton Heath, another south London suburb, which is midway between Croydon and Streatham. All of the people in the car ran off except for one man who remained inside, injured and in need of medical help. His name was Marcel Salami. He was wearing a bullet-proof vest, and an automatic pistol was lying at his feet. Salami told the police that he had been kidnapped and was therefore a victim of crime.

This incident was investigated by a team from Operation Trident. This is an initiative set up by the Metropolitan Police in the late 1990s to tackle shootings and murders committed by black people on fellow blacks. They have not been short of work, and over 300 officers are currently seconded to this unit.

Here are some examples of the types of cases they have had to deal with.

A pregnant mother was driving in her car with her two young children when she became embroiled in a row following a minor accident. Unfortunately for her, the occupant of the car that she had collided with was one Colin Grant. He worked himself up into such a state that he produced a gun and shot the woman quite needlessly in the leg. He got nine years' imprisonment.

Mark Lambie, otherwise known as 'The Prince of Darkness', was once described as Operation Trident's number one target. He had a particular penchant for kidnapping fellow criminals. Thereafter he would torture them with a hammer, a hot iron and boiling water. When he stood trial, he stated that he lived in Streatham. He was jailed for 12 years.

Daniel Cummings was sitting in his car conversing with another motorist, Adrian Crawford. Their conversation degenerated into an argument, so Cummings pulled out a gun and shot Crawford dead. He drove away but was later arrested and convicted. He got life imprisonment.

Despite reassurances continually churned out by police and politicians, many people that I have met during the course of researching these cases have voiced fears and concerns over the proliferation of gun crime. Campaign groups such as Mothers Against Murder and Aggression (MAMAA), and Mothers Against Guns (MAG) have been formed as a result of the destruction that these crimes have caused. MAMAA has given help and support to no less than 400 bereaved families in the past 12 years, and nearly all of those cases involved firearms. They recently held a march in London in memory of 17-year-old murder victim Anton Hyman. He was last seen alive on Saturday, 20 March 2004 in a taxi in Ealing, west London. Some hours later his body was found dumped in a river. He had been repeatedly stabbed, beaten and shot in the back. Young Anton, unlike Jan, had been in trouble with the police before, but surely did not deserve the treatment meted out to him. His killers have never been captured. At the end of the march, relatives and spokespersons for MAMAA made impassioned pleas for stiffer jail sentences for those convicted of gun crime, and for those involved with guns to put down their weapons. I wish them well in their campaign.

The initial focus of Operation Trident was to concentrate on Jamaican immigrant gangsters, who were dealing drugs and protecting their interests with guns – they are widely known as 'Yardies'. This name originated from gangsters in Jamaica who would speak of their territory as their 'yard'. I had the dubious privilege of encountering one such character way back before the days of Trident. Keith Valentine Graham, or 'Levi' as he was known on the streets, was a Jamaican resident of Brixton, south London, who was making a tidy living from dealing most types of drugs but predominantly heroin. He had established links with a group of Africans who were doing the importing and who would then leave the distribution to the fearsome Levi, whose reputation and willingness to use extreme violence ensured that he went about his business largely untroubled.

I was introduced to him in my guise as a bar owner who wanted to supplement his income through drug dealing. Many meetings with him followed during which we would discuss how, where and when we were going to exchange drugs for money. He was also using these meetings to suss me out, to see if I was a genuine drug dealer and not an undercover cop. He would bring an assortment of drugs to these meetings, including cocaine and cannabis, which he smoked almost continuously, and would offer to me. On the first couple of occasions I declined to partake of his drugs, preferring to keep a clear head during the often difficult negotiations. Levi was determined that I should give my money to him and tried to reassure me that he would return later with the large consignment of heroin he was offering. This of course I would not do. He could merely disappear with my cash and never return.

An informant got word back to me that Levi, while he liked me, was becoming increasingly suspicious of my reluctance to take drugs. I did not want this target to slip through the net, so at the next meeting I shared a cannabis joint with him. Then another and another. We sat around for hours, eating vast quantities of pizza and ice cream, slurping gallons of Red Stripe beer, and reciting West Indian poetry on which I suddenly became an authority. Levi regaled me with tales of him shooting people back home in Jamaica, and, stoned as we were, we roared with laughter. Any suspicions he might have had about me vanished and we finally agreed upon a plan as to how we would do the deal.

At the end of this meeting I rang my boss to let him know the plans for the agreed trade that was to take place two days later. He demanded I return to Scotland Yard for a debriefing. I made up an excuse not to attend, which he did not fall for. Finally, I had to say to him, 'Please, Guvnor, I'm rather drunk and off my face through puffing all afternoon. I don't want to come back to the yard and have everybody see me in this state. What if I bump into the commissioner in the lift, he'll think his drug squad is turning into a bunch of dopeheads.' He begrudgingly agreed, so I met a colleague who took me home.

Sober, straight and ready to roll, I met Levi on the day arranged for the exchange. Concealed in the waistband of his trousers, but unbeknown to me, was a fully loaded 9mm automatic pistol. Fortunately he was arrested before he had time to use it, and the following day the police press department was briefed to trumpet the downfall of a man dubbed 'an armed and dangerous Yardie'.

As well as investigating armed incidents, officers from Trident have endeavoured to establish links with police forces in the Caribbean and with London's black communities. The reasons for this include a better exchange of intelligence and information, and to try to gain the confidence of members of black communities in order that people will come forward and give evidence when necessary.

A posting on to Operation Trident is not for the workshy or faint-hearted. The willingness of these criminals to use firearms with increasing disregard for the public is reflected by the fact that most of the incidents Trident investigate involve the firing of weapons in public places.

When Trident officers began to research the crashed BMW in which Marcel Salami had been captured, a possible link to Jan's murder became apparent. The registration number was checked on any potentially relevant police computer database, including the one holding all the information relating to Jan's killing. A positive trace came up. The BMW had been seen on CCTV seized by the murder squad on their swoop of all such cameras in the area. The relevant section of tape was examined, and it showed Salami filling the same car, J11 HSK, with petrol at 2.20am on 12 May, at a Jet garage in Knights Hill, West Norwood. This garage is about half a mile from Valleyfield Road, and this sighting of Salami was only four minutes before Jan was known to have been shot. At this stage in the investigation it was believed that Jan might have driven past this garage on his way home. Believing it to be their best lead yet, the Murder Investigation Team set about thoroughly examining all the tapes in their possession. CCTV taken from a local authority housing estate showed that Jan's BMW had not in fact passed this garage but had driven along Crown Dale in the direction of his home and through a set of traffic lights that controlled the junction with Knights Hill. The timing of these tapes meant the police were able to establish categorically that the BMW Salami had driven out of the Jet garage and Jan's BMW were at this junction at the same time, and only a couple of minutes before he was shot.

Neither the Murder Investigation Team nor the officers from Operation Trident believed Salami's kidnapping story. Neither did the jury who later heard the case against him. The police felt that when all the facts surrounding the nightclub chase were put together with what they knew about Jan's murder, the sighting of Salami and the BMW in the garage could not be merely coincidental.

Two other men, Quincey Thwaites and Junior Reid, were also arrested for their parts in the chase from the nightclub, and all three were considered as suspects for Jan's murder. The CCTV from the garage was inconclusive as to how many other people were with Salami in the car. I have seen the enhanced stills taken from the film and it would appear that another person may be in the rear nearside seat of the BMW, but it is difficult to be certain. All that can be said with certainty is that Salami, who was pictured on this warm evening wearing a short-sleeved shirt and dark trousers, drove that car in and out of the garage. Anything else would be speculative. The police concentrated on him as their main suspect for Jan's murder.

DCI Scola admitted that various tactics were employed to try to extract further information or a possible confession from Salami while he was in custody, but would not expand on what these might have been. I would guess as a matter of pure speculation on my part that his cell was bugged. This is reasonably easy to do in a police station. A minute microphone or transmitter can be concealed in the cell into which a suspect is to be placed. As is the case with many covert police tactics, legal problems can be encountered when trying to have evidence obtained in this way ruled admissible at any later trial.

Another tactic I suspect they may have employed was placing an undercover officer in the same cell as Salami, though again this is just speculation on my part. No evidence from bugging or undercover officers was given in court.

If the police had used someone in the cell, it would have required some forethought and a degree of planning, as legal difficulties can be encountered in having any evidence obtained by the undercover cop allowed in a trial, but it is a method that has been deployed successfully in the past.

This is how such an infiltration can happen. An undercover officer is brought into a police station in the same way as any other arrested person. The arresting officers are sometimes unaware that the person they have arrested is a cop, although it is usually best to have them in on the act. The 'suspect' is booked in by the custody officer, a sergeant who is responsible for the detention of arrested persons. All normal procedures such as the taking of DNA samples, fingerprinting, and the arranging for a legal representative to attend, take place. Many retired cops now work as legal representatives, so it is relatively easy to get a friendly former colleague to be in on the scam. It is often preferable for the fake 'suspect' to be of the same ethnic background as the target and to purport to have something in common with him. It is also useful for the 'suspect' to have been 'arrested' for a serious crime that has some kudos within whatever criminal circles the target may operate.

Additionally, it is often useful for the 'suspect' to have some grievance with the police to discuss with his target, such as having been assaulted (he needs to have the wound to authenticate this!), or having had evidence planted on him, or money stolen from him by the cops. Once all authentic procedures are carried out, the 'suspect' is placed in a cell with the target and left to do his stuff. Invariably the first question asked of a cellmate is, 'What have you been nicked for?' If the planning has been thorough, the answer to this question should be the key that opens up conversation with the suspect. Shared experiences ought to follow. Shared interests and shared knowledge of people and places always help.

On occasions undercover officers have also been placed into a cell inside a prison with a target. This does, however, require a greater number of people to be made aware of the subterfuge, like some of the prison staff, and therefore carries increased risks. Another danger is that it can take a lot longer to extract an undercover officer from a prison than it does from a police station cell, should his real identity ever be discovered by the inmates.

Whatever tactics the police did employ, it appears they did not bring about the results that they hoped for. Of course it may be that Salami had nothing at all to do with Jan's murder, and therefore would have nothing incriminating to say. His sighting at the garage four minutes before and half a mile away from the scene of Jan's shooting may indeed be entirely coincidental. But the police still thought he might know something about it.

They concentrated their search for any potential evidence on the forensic examination of both BMWs. When Jan's car was examined, two small .22 calibre rounds were found to have been fired into the rear of his car; these are believed to have been the first shots fired at him. Neither of them hit Jan but lodged in the large speaker boxes that he had constructed himself from heavy chipboard. It is entirely possible that Jan was not aware that these shots had been fired at him. A witness was found who spoke of hearing loud music coming from a car, possibly Jan's, and it may be that his music drowned out the sound of these shots. If, however, he had known that he was being shot at, I believe he would have taken evasive action. I think that he would have driven his powerful car as fast as he possibly could in order to escape the gunmen who were threatening his life. I do not believe he would have turned into the road where he lived, as it had speed bumps that would have slowed him down or damaged his car.

A large-calibre weapon was used to deliver the fatal shots. The police will only disclose that it is a rare type of gun, a semi-automatic pistol of a make and type not commonly seen on the streets of Britain. Having established that two different types of gun were fired at Jan's car, the police will not be drawn as to the number of gunmen they believe were responsible. I would speculate that two guns equates to two gunmen. The police have also never been able to establish whether they were fired by a person on foot or in a car. What they do know about the rounds fired from the large-calibre weapon is that one round went in through the rear windscreen and another hit the rear driver's-side door. A third hit the post between the driver's door and the rear passenger door, slicing straight through it, and another hit Jan in the head, which proved fatal. I have seen the photographs taken of his car, both at the scene and later at the laboratory, and they do not make pleasant viewing. The blood loss he suffered at the scene was huge, and a piece of brain tissue lying beneath the driver's pedals provided a haunting image, and proved testament to the power of the weapon used.

All these shots hit Jan's car at about the same height, about a metre from the ground, and the number of spent cases found at the scene tallied with the number of rounds that hit his car. I speculated at some length with DCI Scola about where they had been fired from. He was willing to theorise with me, which is an entirely proper way of trying to piece together events, but did not want his theories to be quoted. I would like to put on record my gratitude for his cooperation.

The fatal wound entered the side of Jan's head. I think it reasonable to believe therefore that he was concentrating on where he was going as opposed to looking around. I believe he had slowed down for the speed bump in Valleyfield Road, unaware of the two .22 rounds having been fired. As he slowed down and got close to the kerb in order that only two wheels climbed the bump, I think a vehicle drew closer and that another gunman in the passenger side of this car started to fire. This meant the first large-calibre round hit the rear window. I believe the gunman continued to fire as his car moved forward, essentially manoeuvring in order to eventually pass Jan's car. Hence the rounds entered Jan's car from the rear to the front, and, as their car drew level with Jan's, the fatal round was fired. Then I think his almost lifeless body became a dead weight, causing his right foot to slump down on to the accelerator, propelling the car through the garden wall. The entire shooting incident may have happened in only a few seconds, and I doubt Jan would have become aware of what was happening before it was too late.

The forensic examination of Jan's car was not able to establish from what distance these rounds had been fired. The examination of the other BMW, the car in which Salami had been seen on that fatal night and which he was arrested in some 17 days later, did not reveal any forensic evidence tying it to Jan's murder. The weapon found at Salami's feet could not be connected to Jan's murder.

Despite this the murder squad were still convinced that Salami was in some way connected. They decided to hold another press conference. They were going to use a very different tactic. On 26 June 2001, DCI Pandolfi said the police would like to hear from anyone who might have been in or around the Jet garage at 2.20am on 12 May and who might have seen the seven series BMW being filled with petrol. He also said he would like to hear from anyone who might have seen an incident involving Jan's distinctive black BMW and a grey BMW, or any other car, near Knights Hill or along Crown Lane, or anywhere along the route to Jan's home in Valleyfield Road.

There was then a rather unusual announcement. It was

revealed that the Metropolitan Police Service, through the Director of Intelligence, who is a very senior detective, was offering a reward of £7,500 and that payment of this reward was not dependent upon charge and conviction of those responsible but could be paid out if any information given moved the investigation forward substantially.

Of course 'substantially' is open to interpretation in many ways, and the judge of that would ultimately be the Director of Intelligence, but this was an innovative move on behalf of the police. The problem with offering rewards that are subject to conviction is that an informant may offer up information upon which the police act, charging a suspect, only to see them acquitted because a jury are not convinced 'beyond reasonable doubt' of their guilt or because of some other issue that arises during the trial. These issues are sometimes impossible for prosecutors to anticipate, or simply arise as a trial twists and turns this way and that as they are often prone to do. Witnesses can perform better or worse than expected or can change their story, or simply not turn up. New evidence can be introduced which may alter the case for either prosecution or defence, or any number of often complicated legal issues can arise. Countless volumes of legal textbooks detail these issues, and, law being the ever-evolving beast that it is, legal precedents are set on an almost daily basis.

An acquittal can result in an informant who supplied the information, and who may have backed it up by giving evidence in court thereby putting themselves at considerable risk, seeing their chances of getting any reward money disappear.

This is in stark contrast to the way in which tens of thousands of pounds were paid out to my former informants. Most of these would come to me and say, for example, 'John Smith, who lives at 123 Acacia Avenue is going to be driving a lorry-load of drugs, guns, stolen goods or whatever, up the M1 to Birmingham tomorrow.' This of course is a very simplified example. It was rarely as easy as that! We would carry out surveillance on John Smith, and duly arrest him and seize the contraband.

Almost immediately I would submit a report to my supervisors applying for my informant to be rewarded. I would have checked out previously the informant's motives and role in the crime and established that he had not set the whole thing up, and was therefore eligible for a reward. This report would make its way up the chain of command until reaching an officer of sufficient rank who could authorise whatever reward he or she saw fit. Sometimes the bosses would arrive at a figure that we felt did not accurately reflect the amount of danger the informant had faced, or the amount of time and effort he or she had put into getting us our vital leads. On these occasions we would have to make clear such details and resubmit the report. Mostly the bosses would be sympathetic and increase the reward money, which would then be paid out. There was no requirement for criminal convictions in these cases because we all knew that the risk of acquittal is a fact of life – it happens.

This system was open to abuse, but we were most careful in ensuring that we were not simply being used by these informants to arrest whoever they wanted. By and large the system worked. It encouraged people to come forward and they very rarely had to give evidence because we had already obtained enough. They liked the money and we got our results. Everybody was happy except the bad guys.

This offer from the Metropolitan Police in relation to Jan's killing showed they were willing to be flexible. Although it has not yet brought them the result they hoped for, and despite the fact this is the smallest reward I have come across in any of the cases in this book, the cash is still available today and the same conditions apply. Bearing in mind it is over four years since they made the offer, if anybody has any such information, I would suggest they approach a solicitor and ask him to try to negotiate the figure up, to take into account inflation and the current stagnation of the investigation. It has got to be worth a go.

Back in the devastated Aylward family, Alan was trying to keep Jan's pet shop business afloat. He told me, 'I worked there every day for a few weeks after the shooting. I had little old ladies coming in who couldn't believe what had happened. Through them I learned about a different side to him. He was a young man who didn't necessarily want his dad to think he was a soft touch, but these ladies used to come in and tell me how Jan would give their dogs a free chew and they all thought he was such a nice boy. It's not until something like this happens that you find out how other people saw him and how much they liked him. People were wonderful to me. They were very supportive and put signs up asking for witnesses. But it was a really difficult time. I was in a right state after what had happened and yet I had to explain it all time and time again, because every second customer that came in was shocked and wanted to know the details. We eventually sold the business to a customer.'

DCI Pandolfi decided to take the case to *Crimewatch*. A reconstruction was aired on Wednesday, 18 July. Alan made an appearance but was a little disappointed that in the cauldron that is live television some points that were going to be raised were not. However the phones did ring. DCI Pandolfi made another public appeal soon after the programme went out. He said, 'A number of calls were received and were very helpful, but one was particularly important. Soon after the appeal was broadcast a caller rang in to the programme and spoke to a detective for nearly 15 minutes. They gave a lot of interesting information and we need them to contact us again. I can promise them their information will be treated in the strictest confidence, and that everyone who approaches us will be treated with the utmost care and sensitivity.'

The quest for information in relation to this case continues to this day. But DCI Scola has told me the investigation has been looked at by the Murder Review Group, a part of the Metropolitan Police that examines unsolved murder investigations after 28 days, and that the case has officially been 'put away'. That means to say it is not now investigated on a daily basis, but judging by the intelligence reports I noticed on his desk, fresh information continues to come in. The police have a stock saying that goes 'a murder case is never closed', but the harsh reality is that there are so many cases and there is only so much that they believe can be done. Some investigations are very much closed. This case, however, is not one of them. In fact I was told that they were in possession of some recent information that I could not be made privy to as it was linked to another 'job' – police speak for another murder.

In March 2002, Marcel Salami, Quincey Thwaites and Junior Reid stood trial for firearms offences at the Old Bailey. Salami gave an address in Peckham, south London, Thwaites said he was of no fixed address, and Reid gave an address in

Northampton. It is my understanding that they were all believed to be living in Brixton at the time of the incidents for which they were standing trial.

Salami and Thwaites were charged with possession of firearms with intent to endanger life on 28 May 2001. These charges related to an allegation that they had both fired a number of shots in a Brixton street in connection with a running feud that they had had with some fellow hoodlums.

Salami, Thwaites and Reid were all charged with possession of firearms with intent to endanger life on 29 May 2001 – these charges related to the police chase from the Croydon nightclub.

They all pleaded 'not guilty' to all charges, and the trial began. The police officers involved in the chase were unable to say who fired which weapon, not surprising perhaps seeing as they were dodging bullets from automatic weapons while driving at breakneck speed. Had they been able to be specific, then charges of attempted murder may have been preferred. In any event, Salami, Thwaites and Reid were all convicted and jailed.

The presiding judge, Jeremy Roberts, sentenced Salami to ten years, and commended three police constables, Craig Birkhead, Bob Brown and Dave Winton, for their bravery and professionalism. Detective Superintendent Barry Phillips from Operation Trident, the officer who had led the inquiry into the nightclub chase and who had liaised closely with the officers investigating Jan's murder, was delighted with the outcome. He said, 'This sends out a strong message to those who choose to live by the gun. It is a major success for Operation Trident.'

The murder investigation continued irrespective of the jailing of Salami. At least now detectives would have no problem finding him if they ever wanted to re-interview him. I have written to him in jail asking for an interview, but I have not received a reply. Detectives wanted to see him sooner than he might have expected.

The inquest into Jan's death was to be heard. Unusually it was not held at a coroner's court but at Southwark Crown Court, a building that normally hears criminal trials and consequently has a considerably higher level of security. The coroner, Mrs Selena Lynch, began hearing the evidence. Suddenly, surprised and clearly less than impressed, Marcel Salami was put in front of her. He had been brought from his cell in HMP Parkhurst without being informed where he was going or why. It was hoped that this surprise tactic might catch him off guard and get him to offer up previously undisclosed facts.

Before he spoke he was reminded of his right that he did not have to say anything that might incriminate himself, and the questions from the coroner began. She asked, 'Did you have anything to do with Mr Aylward's killing?' He replied, 'When I was first interviewed, I told police I know nothing about this.'

The coroner continued, 'Did you know anyone else who might be responsible for his death?' Salami said, 'I don't know anything.' Mrs Lynch further asked, 'Did you have a BMW? Did you have a firearm in your car?' Salami angrily retorted, 'I don't see why I should answer this. I don't know nothing.'

Mrs Lynch may have thought any further questioning a waste of time, in any event she asked him no more questions, and he was taken out of the court and back to prison.

The final witnesses and evidence were heard, including testimony from Alan Aylward. A verdict of unlawful killing was returned, and Mrs Lynch had some words for those assembled, including the Aylward family. She said, 'I very much hope that this man's killer or killers are brought to justice, and the fact that we are concluding this inquest today does not give anyone a hiding place. I'm so sorry for your loss. You have learned that time isn't really a healer, and I do sincerely hope that one day you will see someone brought to justice for his death.' I could not agree more.

I asked DCI Scola what it would take for that to happen now, some four years on. 'We need a witness,' he said. He continued, 'I would still encourage anyone with information to come and speak to us. I am confident that with our experienced witness protection unit, and the fact that witnesses are being protected more and more by the courts now with screens and the like, that we could solve this.' I told him that the telephone number previously issued for this inquiry was now unobtainable, and he gave me the new number – 020 8721 4111.

Alan Aylward told me his current feelings. 'Where we lived was a quiet enclave of Streatham. Sure there were problems that we'd heard of in other parts of Streatham and in Brixton, but we didn't expect this sort of thing to happen where we lived. After Jan died, his brother, who is only three years younger than Jan, was devastated. They were mates and did a lot of things together. He has never really got over it. I thought I had, but doing this interview has reminded me that I haven't. His brother still lives in south London in not the most upmarket of areas, and I have to try hard not to worry too much about him. I wish he would move somewhere else, but he enjoys it down there [Alan moved out to Surrey after Jan's murder as the pain of living in the road where it happened was too much to bear]. I'm frustrated with life. Whoever did this are just thugs; I would like to see them caught and punished but I recognise that life doesn't always bring you what you want. But at the end of the day it won't bring him back. My frustration is that it happened in the first place. You don't think it is going to happen to your family, and you don't understand why it does when it does. I'm frustrated with life and how it turns out.'

I bade him farewell and made my way to his front door, passing photos of Jan and other family members. My mind went back to the first time I had met Alan. That was in central London and I had passed a busker singing a tune by the pop group Tears for Fears. It was called 'Mad World'.

CHAPTER TEN

UNRESOLVED

The Law Commission is a body that advises the government on law reform. They published a report on 6 August 2004 in which they described the law in relation to murder as 'a mess'. In October that year the Home Office announced that a review of murder law would take place, the first such review for 40 years. In June 2005, some newspapers began to speculate about the findings of that review and claimed that sources had informed them that changes to sentencing would be made, and that the mandatory life sentence for murder would be abolished. However, the Home Secretary Charles Clarke made it clear that he wanted to retain mandatory life sentences. On 16 June 2005, the solicitor general told the House of Commons, 'The government's key responsibility is to ensure that we maintain confidence in the criminal justice system, protect victims and bring the guilty to justice.'

The previous nine chapters in this book have dealt with cases where no person has yet been charged with those murders. I was keen to research a case where somebody had been charged.

Woolwich in south London is a living, breathing, pulsating example of Britain's 21st-century multicultural society. During the day the high street and markets are populated by people with origins from every corner of the Earth. This is reflected in the local businesses, and a few hours spent here can broaden your knowledge of many things.

I used to be taken to Woolwich when I was a child; my mother used to hunt for bargains in the famous covered market, as she could clothe my sister and me for considerably less than it would cost in our home town. Now, some 30 years on, the market boasts cut-price merchandise of a different nature. It is possible to kit yourself out in the latest fashions made popular by hip-hop and rap music performers, and you can buy the CDs to go with your new look. You may wish to sample some Thai food, buy some discount furniture, or have your hair put into corn rows. As I mingled with the shoppers I saw men in robes and women in burkas, and it was impossible to ignore the many different dialects and accents that I could hear all around me.

I paused outside a grocer's shop, quizzically examining vegetables from around the world that I had not previously encountered. The proprietor soon approached me and kindly gave me a lesson in cooking chow chow, white aubergine and bitter melon, which I now know is beneficial for people who suffer from diabetes. Outside a pet shop I saw some young men conversing while their fearsome-looking bull terriers strained at their leashes.

In among the food and clothing stalls I found a Christian bookshop that sold bibles and many other theological writings, along with framed pictures of Christ and a scroll listing the Ten Commandments. Number six reads, 'Thou shalt not kill.'

Terry Gregory was only 19 years old when he was killed. He worked as a lifeguard at Eltham swimming pools and was described to me by customers and others who knew him as an outstanding young man. Other words used were sociable, popular and conscientious, and apparently he was the sort of person who did not wait to be asked for help but would actively seek out customers who he thought could benefit from his expertise. He was very fit, worked out every day and harboured ambitions to further his career in the leisure industry. He was single and still lived in the family home.

The pools where he worked closed for two weeks over the Christmas holiday period of 2003. So on the night of Saturday, 27 December, with no work to go to the following day, Terry decided to go out for a few drinks. With him were his girlfriend 16-year-old Louise Reed and a friend Sam Nelson, who, like Terry, was 19. They went to the Pullman pub in Woolwich, which has a DJ employed on Friday and Saturday nights to play music for the young and lively crowd it attracts. They had a good time and by the time they left Terry was happy, if a touch inebriated. Together they caught the N1 night bus, which should have taken them the ten-minute ride home to nearby Charlton.

Not long into the journey Terry began to feel unwell and decided to get off the bus for some fresh air. Louise and Sam joined him, and as Terry alighted he saw an umbrella lying unattended at the bus stop. He picked it up and was apparently playing around with it when he was confronted by a black man who claimed ownership of it on behalf of one of three female companions that he was with. Accounts of what happened next vary from a row, to an altercation, to an argument, to a fist fight. In any event, as this was going on, a black BMW car stopped and some young Asian men got out and tried to calm matters. They appeared to be successful in defusing matters and went on their way. The black man and his companions got on to the bus that Terry, Louise and Sam had been travelling on and disappeared.

Thinking that the incident was now over, Terry, Louise, and Sam continued walking home. By now it was about 1.30am on Sunday morning, 28 December. They walked for a few minutes along Woolwich Church Street and were apparently approaching the Albion pub, not far from Terry's home, when the black man from the umbrella incident reappeared. In the next few moments Sam suffered a serious knife wound to his hand, and Terry was stabbed nine times, including two wounds in his back. These knife blows caused an injury to his liver, one in his lower body that was delivered with such force that it chipped his hipbone, and a deep stab wound to his heart. As he lay bleeding profusely a distraught Louise cradled him in her arms, and a badly wounded Sam went off to get help. A good Samaritan, Steve Nelson, stopped his car and gave all the assistance he could. An ambulance arrived and the police descended upon the scene and taped off the road. Traffic diversions were put in place and during the commotion many local residents, including the staff of the Albion, were woken up.

Terry was rushed to hospital but doctors were unable to save his life. A murder inquiry was launched and Detective Chief Inspector Lee Catlin made a public appeal. A description of a man wanted for questioning was circulated. On 30 December, a 65-year-old retired man from the Charlton area, George

Edwin, gave himself up to police at Shooters Hill police station. He was questioned in the presence of a solicitor and then charged with Terry's murder and with causing grievous bodily harm to Sam. He was kept in custody until 1 January 2004 when he appeared at Camberwell Green Magistrates Court. At this hearing he was further remanded to appear at the Central Criminal Court, more commonly known as the Old Bailey, in March. At this appearance he entered pleas of 'not guilty' to both charges. A date was fixed for the trial, but, much to the surprise of Terry's family, the case was not to be tried at the Old Bailey but in court one of the Inner London Crown Court.

When I was in the police I was involved in many cases at this court. It is very old and grand, complete with oak panelling, a high ceiling and an elevated position from where the judge presides. An increased workload over the years has meant that other local buildings have been purchased and converted into courts, and some of these are little more than prefabricated huts and not the sort of places where you would expect serious criminal trials to be heard and justice dispensed. On one occasion in court one I was giving evidence of an undercover role I had performed. A well-known team of cocaine distributors and firearms suppliers had become friendly with one of my informants, and he had negotiated himself into a position whereby he could introduce potential buyers of drugs to them. I duly met the bad guys and spent many weeks earning their trust until I was able to place a large order of cocaine with them. After many frantic last-minute changes of plans and negotiations, they finally delivered a large consignment to me. A few months later five defendants stood trial.

As is still often the case, the judge presiding over the trial was no fan of undercover policing tactics. I think he felt that undercover equated to underhand, and I did not expect an easy time of it. After a lot of legal argument and the opening speech by the prosecution barrister had been heard, it was time for me to start my evidence. I took the oath and scanned the jury. I could not believe what I saw, for there staring at me in disbelief was a friend's girlfriend, who knew nothing of my secret life undercover and with whom I had been dancing at a wedding reception less than 48 hours before. What was I to do? Keep quiet and hope she would be able to do the same while engendering support from her fellow jurors for guilty verdicts, or declare straight away to the court that I knew her and thereby ensure a new jury would be sworn in to hear the case. I chose the latter. A few days later I met her in our local pub. She was not pleased that I had been responsible for having her, and therefore all the other members of that jury, removed from a trial that they had decided would be 'juicy'. They had already agreed on guilty verdicts, having only heard the prosecution opening speech. Apparently they had decided that the police would not go to all the bother of infiltrating this bunch of renegades if they weren't up to something.

A second jury was sworn in and some of them were later nobbled by associates of those on trial as they made their way home from court over the weeks that it took for all the evidence to be heard. They and their families were threatened with violence if they did not acquit the defendants, which only came to light when the 'not guilty' verdicts had been delivered and a tearful and apologetic female juror confessed what had happened to my colleague. We all trudged away unhappy with how that trial had ended.

If I and my former colleagues had felt hard done by on that occasion, it was nothing compared to the frustration and anger felt by Terry Gregory's family and friends when they left that same building in November 2004.

Stewart Rigby is a very pleasant man to spend time with. His reasoning of matters that interest him is considered, well researched and politely delivered. He has been retired for six years from his work as a market research executive for the British Tourist Authority. He lives in Lewisham, another multicultural part of south London not dissimilar to Woolwich, and when his local swimming pool closed he decided to try out the facilities at Eltham pools. Stewart swims regularly as he suffers from Marfan's syndrome. This condition can affect the main artery from the heart, so exercise is important for his continued wellbeing. Another consequence of this condition is that Stewart's arm span is greater than his height. He stands six-foot ten and his arm span is seven-foot one, so he needs more room in which to swim than your average person. Terry Gregory, when seeing Stewart prepare to enter the pool, would automatically widen the roped off area set aside for adult lane swimming that Stewart used.

On one occasion Stewart decided to approach Terry and thank him for his considerate and customer-friendly behaviour. They spoke regularly to one another thereafter. On 29 December 2003, a friend telephoned Stewart and alerted him to an article in that day's edition of the *Times*. It told of Terry's murder. 'I was very shocked and spoke to a colleague of Terry's at the leisure centre and he confirmed it. It was so horribly true. I went to his funeral and I thought I would go to the trial of the man who had handed himself in to see justice done.'

I asked Stewart if he had had any previous dealings with the criminal justice system in this country, and he told me that his one prior experience had been when he sat as a juror on a trial at the Old Bailey not long after his retirement. This case involved an allegation of attempted murder that arose from an altercation between some Somalis and Bangladeshis in Southall. A large knife was said to have been used, but most of Stewart's fellow jurors saw this matter as six of one and half a dozen of the other, and eventually majority opinion prevailed, and a 'not guilty' verdict was returned.

Stewart sat through every day of the trial of George Edwin, which began on 2 August 2004. Judge Jonathan Van der Werff presided. The first witness for the prosecution was the pathologist who had performed the post-mortem on Terry. The knife used to kill him has never been found, but she estimated that the blade would have been about ten centimetres long. Sam Nelson appeared and much of his evidence was strongly challenged by the defence barrister. During the trial Edwin elected to go into the witness box and stated that Terry had winded him during the event involving the umbrella. He further said that when he saw Terry, Sam and Louise approaching him again a few minutes later he feared he would be attacked. He said this was not outside the Albion pub but some 200 metres away near a road called Prospect Vale. He admitted to being in possession of a knife, which he further admitted drawing from his pocket in an effort to frighten off the three people who were approaching him.

The Crown Prosecution Service had not included a charge of 'possessing a bladed article in a public place' on the list of charges Edwin was to face. This offence was created by the

Criminal Justice Act of 1988, and had been introduced in an effort to combat the increasing number of offenders who were taking knives on to the streets of Britain. For a person to be found guilty of such an offence it must be proved that they were in a place to which the public had access, and that the bladed article that they had in their possession had a blade longer than 7.62 centimetres. I suspect in this case such a charge was not included as Edwin faced much more serious charges and that it could have been perceived as using a sledgehammer to crack a nut. The maximum punishment for this type of offence is two years' imprisonment.

Edwin denied stabbing Terry. He told the court that he had lived in the Woolwich area for the past 40 years and that he did not have any criminal convictions. Once all the evidence had been heard, much of which had been contradictory, the jury retired to consider their verdicts. They were unable to reach verdicts upon which they all agreed. They were further unable to reach verdicts upon which a majority of ten of them agreed, and after much deliberation they were discharged by the judge and a new trial was ordered.

This began on 21 October 2004. Once again Stewart Rigby was in attendance. The same judge oversaw proceedings and the same defence barrister was employed, but the prosecution had a new man at the helm. Terry's young girlfriend Louise Reed had appeared at the first trial in person but had been deeply traumatised by the events. At this trial she gave evidence via a video link but was still subject to a rigorous cross-examination. It was decided that the jury should make a visit to the alleged scene of the attack, and when they arrived it was pointed out to them that the Albion pub sign depicted Winston Churchill as the mythical John Bull, an 18th century character that was supposed to embody the British spirit, an image completed by the wearing of a Union Jack waistcoat. Lying nearby was a floral tribute to Terry, also in the colours and style of a Union Jack. This had been placed there in his honour by a local lady, not long after Britain's Olympic winners had paraded their medals around London. Terry was a sports fanatic and this was how she chose to innocently remember him. When everybody returned to court much was made of this, as if to imply that race was an issue in the fatal events. Terry was a young man born and raised in a multicultural environment with friends from many different races.

Edwin again gave evidence and said he did not remember much of what had happened. This time the jury reached a verdict in relation to the charge of grievous bodily harm on Sam Nelson. They found Edwin not guilty. They could not, however, agree a verdict in relation to the charge of murdering Terry. A majority of them could still not agree after further deliberation. When it became apparent that no amount of time would assist the jury, they were discharged. The Crown Prosecution Service asked the judge for time to consider their position. They were granted two days, and on 3 November all parties reconvened at the court. The prosecution informed the judge that they did not intend to seek a third trial. As a result the judge dismissed the murder charge against George Edwin, declared him not guilty, and discharged him from the court as a free man. He told Edwin, 'You leave this court without a stain upon your character.'

The police officers involved in the case struggled to hide their disappointment, though there was never a suggestion that

Edwin was wrongly acquitted. A statement was released which said, 'All lines of inquiry have been exhausted.'

Stewart Rigby was so outraged by what he saw during these trials and what he believes to be failings in the criminal justice system that he has begun a one-man campaign calling for changes in the law. He has entered into dialogue with the Crown Prosecution Service and various politicians in an effort to get answers to many questions he believes this case raised. He told me, 'I am trying to get the people who are in power, through my MP, to admit that there is something not right about the jury system. I can see the advantages of it, but in murder cases where people from different races are involved, emotions and prejudice can be stirred up which deflects people's attention from the evidence. It doesn't apply merely to race issues, issues of age or gender can be used in the same way, and I just don't trust juries to make up their minds on the evidence put before them without being distracted. I'm not saying that I know better than the common man or woman who would serve on a jury, but, as much as a judge may ask a jury just to concentrate only upon the evidence they have heard, it must be very difficult for them when numerous unfounded and uncorroborated allegations are made about a dead man who cannot answer for himself.'

As he acknowledges, it's not possible to know what influences any particular jury. In this case, race may not have had anything at all to do with Edwin's acquittal. Nevertheless, Stewart continued, 'In the second trial the prosecution barrister gave a most academic, intellectual, precise and analytical presentation; at the time I thought it was very good. But the defence barrister again hinted and suggested things about the character of the victim without being challenged. I am not a legal expert, and if my thoughts are clouded as a result, then I would of course rethink my views and position. But at the moment I am just hitting a brick wall in my efforts to get answers to my questions from the people who run the system.' He is, however, determined to carry on until he gets some answers, and is currently corresponding with the Home Office minister, the Right Honourable Baroness Scotland of Asthal, QC, known to her friends as Patricia. At the foot of her letters the current Home Office line appears, which reads, 'Building a safe, just and tolerant society.'

Stewart's latest letter from the Home Office informed him of the government's recently announced review of the law on murder and manslaughter, something of which he was well aware. Perhaps those in power should consult laymen such as him in order to hear the views and concerns of the man on the street who has actually witnessed criminal trials.

One area of the law upon which his thinking is accurate concerns the rules that govern the directions a judge can give to a jury when considering a charge of murder. The senior crown prosecutor who handled the Terry Gregory case has confirmed this to him in writing. As the law stands, a jury that is deciding the guilt or innocence of somebody charged with murder cannot be asked to consider an alternative verdict of manslaughter until they agree either way upon the murder charge. Suppose I was standing trial for the murder of somebody I had allegedly beaten to death. The jury may all believe that I killed that person unlawfully, but be divided as to whether it was premeditated – that is to say 'with malice aforethought'. As a result of their inability to agree a verdict on the murder charge, they would not be allowed to consider a verdict on manslaughter and I could walk free, even though they all believed I was responsible for that person's death.

Another member of the public who has expressed her concerns about the criminal justice system more publicly than most is Roberta Woods. This south-London-based mother of two teenage children told me of her experiences as a juror. 'Several years ago I did jury service at Southwark Crown Court,' she said. 'I was happy to do this but the experience left me totally disillusioned with the justice system in this country. I sat as a juror on three or four trials and found that my fellow jurors, just ordinary individuals with no background in the law, took their roles really seriously. Their greatest fear is finding someone guilty who is innocent. That is fine, but in order to ensure they did not make such a mistake they would rather believe any allegation that the police planted evidence or were otherwise in the wrong, or that the victim in some way deserved whatever happened to him. It ended up with the police and victims being on trial rather than the defendants; they would end up being portrayed by their barristers as victims of some misfortune or another. Only one of the trials I sat on ended in a conviction. In one case the defendant went sick, in another they were acquitted. Even in the case where we convicted, it was remanded for some psychiatric reports or something, so we didn't see justice dispensed.

'Then in 2004 I was summonsed for jury service once again. The timing clashed with my final exams for my degree course, and in any event I didn't think I was going to make a good juror because you are supposed to be objective and impartial and after my previous experience I knew I couldn't be. I wrote to the jury-summoning officer and stated why I would not make a good juror, that I had no faith in the system. They wrote back to me saying that my reasons weren't good enough and that I would have to turn up. They did say, however, that I could put my case to a judge on the day. I duly presented myself and went to see a judge but he ruled that I would have to serve. The jury-summoning officer said she sympathised with me and promised to get me on a short case and then release me.

'Straight away I got called to a case, sworn in, and it began. An Asian man was charged with threatening to kill another Asian man, and there were allegations of a knife being used. Both victim and defendant spoke through interpreters. This slowed proceedings down no end, yet one of them would answer questions before they had been interpreted, so it seemed clear to me he could understand English. After an hour of this I could stand it no longer, so I got up and said out loud to the court, 'I'm not going to watch this rubbish any more,' and walked out. I'm not normally given to such sort of displays, but I could not stand watching another re-enactment of the same sort of rubbish I had seen years previously. The clerk of the court was less than pleased with me and said to me in the lobby, "Do you realise you could go to prison for this?" I came home and the following day a summons arrived ordering me back to court to answer a charge of contempt.

'I was put in front of a different judge, who said to me, "Do you realise how much tax payer's money you have wasted?" He went on to say that my actions had cost £8,000. I presumed this to be the cost for the hour of court time that I had disrupted, and the swearing in of a new jury etc. I said my piece and then he fined me £300. He told me to pay within a month or face seven days in jail. There was no option of doing community service or any other non-custodial sentence. I thought I may be being punished more harshly than a defendant whose guilt or innocence I had been asked to decide.'

Roberta believes the jury system should be replaced. 'Defendants always opt for jury trial because they know jurors will turn themselves inside out to find them not guilty. Trivial matters should certainly not be tried in front of a jury, and nor should serious matters such as murder. I see no benefit in the jury system whatsoever. I would prefer a system similar to that in France where they have an examining magistrate.'

While Terry's family and friends tried to come to terms with their continuing grief and the intense frustration that they felt because no person had been found responsible for his death, some people tried to exploit his murder for political purposes. The far right National Front (NF) held a wreath-laying service at the scene of Terry's murder in January 2004. This had been against the wishes of his mother Sue and many others. They did not want Terry's memory to be blighted by association to a group with extreme views. The NF went ahead regardless, and Sue voiced her disquiet through the local press. A year later the NF planned another wreath laying, preceded by a march. They entitled it a 'Stop racist attacks' demonstration, and urged supporters to meet outside Woolwich Dockyard railway station at noon on Saturday, 13 January 2005. From there they intended to walk to the Albion pub and lay flowers, followed by a minute's silence.

Meanwhile an organisation from the opposite side of the political spectrum, Unite Against Fascism, also urged their followers to assemble at the railway station in an effort to stop the march. Numerous uniformed police officers awaited the arrival of both groups. The NF summoned up 25 followers, while Unite Against Fascism did rather better with a head count of 80. The NF demonstrators carried large Union flags, and many sported very short haircuts. Some chose to cover their faces with scarves. Their opponents carried banners urging, 'Stop the fascist BNP', referring to the British National Party. The NF marchers set off much to the disappointment of Unite Against Fascism, and as they progressed many onlookers stood and gazed. Some seemed bemused by it all, while some passing motorists tooted their horns in apparent support of the marchers. Local press photographers snapped away, as did one of the NF demonstrators. When they got to the scene of the attack on Terry, Bernard Franklin, the Deputy Chairman of the NF, laid flowers, took a pace backwards, bowed and then began the minute's silence. A copy of what the NF calls the 'fallen list' was placed on the pavement. This is a list of white victims who the NF claim are victims of racist murders. Terry Blackham, a prominent member of the NF, then delivered a speech about racist attacks on white people.

Less than three miles from this spot, in Well Hall Road, Eltham, there is a plaque set in the pavement that remembers another teenage murder victim. It reads 'In memory of Stephen Lawrence 13.9.1974 to 22.4.1993. May he rest in peace.' The stabbing to death of this young black man has haunted the Metropolitan Police for over a decade, and will continue to do so for some time. At the inquest into Stephen's death, the police investigation was lambasted for a number of errors and omissions. The then Home Secretary Jack Straw set up the McPherson inquiry, which was tasked with examining in detail the actions of the police. As well as ripping huge holes in the investigation, the inquiry famously branded the Metropolitan Police as 'institutionally racist'. The impact of this on the Met was huge and has not been helped by the fact that no one has ever been convicted of this crime. Five white youths were charged with Stephen's murder as a result of a prosecution brought by his family. Three were sent for trial but acquitted when the trial collapsed. Two subsequent police investigations have failed to obtain any fresh evidence upon which to charge anyone. There are still officers working on the case today, 12 years after the murder.

So here we have two south London teenage murder victims, one black and one white, both stabbed to death, and nobody convicted of either crime. I spoke to a middle-aged trader who has lived in Woolwich for the past 42 years after emigrating from Pakistan, and I asked him if these cases had any effect on him. 'Oh, yes, very much so,' he said. 'Woolwich is a multi-cultural place and for people to live happily side-by-side it is important that justice is seen to be done. When it is not, it fails us all and puts further pressure on the community as a whole. And it is not only the big cases that need to be resolved. People want justice from whoever is dealing with a grievance. For example, if someone has a complaint with someone in the local council over a business, say their rates, they want what they perceive as justice. If someone makes a complaint to the police, which is very hard to do as they never walk anywhere, they just screech around in cars with lights flashing and sirens blasting, they want that matter dealt with and not brushed aside as they tend to do round here. All these things are perceived as justice matters, and when people see justice being denied in big newsworthy and local cases they think, What chance have I the little man got with my complaint or problem? This in turn leads to people being attracted to extremist politics. And people who get involved in extremist politics use this place to further their own aims by stirring up conflict and discontent. Justice is so vitally important.'

I went to meet Sue Gregory at her home. I wanted to get her opinion upon matters. She made me most welcome and proudly showed me photos, certificates and other memorabilia of Terry's life. I couldn't help but be mightily impressed by the resilience and fortitude she displayed throughout our time together. Her complaints about the criminal justice system were numerous, and many of those grievances are identical to those of Stewart Rigby. She was also angry that some areas of the court were used by the defendants, their friends and relatives, as well as by people connected to the victims.

On a slightly different note, Sue was dismayed that no CCTV footage had been available from the bus on which Terry and his companions had travelled. Apparently it was not working that night, and she, like me, cannot see the point of these systems being installed if they are not going to serve the purpose for which they were conceived. This is not an isolated case. From a previous chapter you will recall the same occurred with a system at Walton on Thames railway station; those cameras, had they been working, may have captured images relevant to the disappearance of Milly Dowler.

On a personal front, the effect of Terry's killing on Sue has been cataclysmic. Her marriage has broken up and she now battles to support her remaining family. She told me, 'None of us are the same people since it happened. I am holding the family together for my children and grandchildren. I punish myself for not getting Terry a new dog. I think if I had then he might not have gone out that night. I have nightmares, but in them I believe that Terry is telling me something, so I will never give up until I get some justice for him. After all, you don't bring children into the world, love them, bring them up, only to see them go out one night and not come back.'